I'm Irish
Get Me Out of Here!

Donal Ruane

Gill & Macmillan

For my mother, the coolest chick I know

Gill & Macmillan Ltd
Hume Avenue, Park West, Dublin 12
with associated companies throughout the world
www.gillmacmillan.ie
© Donal Ruane 2004
0 7171 3861 5
Print origination by TypeIT, Dublin
Printed by AIT Nørhaven A/S, Denmark

This book is typeset in 12pt AGaramond on 14.5pt

*The paper used in this book comes from the wood pulp of managed forests.
For every tree felled, at least one tree is planted,
thereby renewing natural resources.*

A CIP catalogue record for this book is available from the
British Library.

3 5 4 2

Contents

v   ACKNOWLEDGEMENTS

1   PROLOGUE

6   THE DRINK THING

43   THE INFRASTRUCTURE THING

69   THE PROPERTY THING

100   THE RACISM THING

118   THE TRIBUNALS THING

148   THE HAPPINESS THING

214   EPILOGUE

Acknowledgements

I didn't necessarily expect to be doing this again, so I more or less got it all out in the acknowledgements section of my first book (now probably available in your better class of remainder shop). Thank God, all those referred to before are still knocking about, so once again, I'd like to express my thanks to each and every one of them for their continued support as I doggedly pursue the old income-without-a-career thing.

Writing this book was at times quite enjoyable, and at other times, something of a pain in the arse. This was principally because before I set out to discuss the state of the nation as we find it today, I was politely counselled to make at least some effort to present my views in a rational, libel-free and reasonably balanced manner. As those who know me will quickly attest to, this approach presented quite a challenge, consequently rendering the completion of this book a decidedly more arduous task than I had initially bargained for when I casually acquiesced to its commission. Ironically enough, what helped me get to the finish line was reading, and in some cases rereading, loads of other people's books when I should have been writing my own, and so I'd just like to acknowledge their indirect contribution.

In no particular order, they are: Jeffrey Eugenides, Paul Auster, David Sedaris, Tim O'Brien, Michael Chabon, Stephen Wright, David Foster Wallace, Tim Winton, Alain de Botton, Geoff Dyer, Patrick McGrath, Christopher Brokmyre, Jonathan Coe, Ian McEwan, Keith Ridgway and DBC Pierre.

Prologue

The idea for this book came out of a very pleasant lunch enjoyed by yours truly and my editor from Gill & Macmillan in DaVincenzo's on Upper Leeson Steeet. Suitably sated, I was just five minutes into my pitch, waxing lyrical about what I thought were two great ideas involving many months of foreign travel at G&M's expense, when the somewhat stony stare from across the table confirmed to me that my 'great' ideas were not in fact garnering the enthusiasm and approval I had perhaps naïvely expected they would. Now suitably chastened, I shut up for a few minutes and listened to the altogether more realistic suggestions proffered by someone with twenty years' experience skippering the choppy seas of the publishing world.

He suggested I write something about the last ten years or so in Irish life, a period which had seen the country make a quantum leap in its efforts to become a thriving, dynamic and confident market economy at the heart of Europe, and how yet, despite our new-found affluence and sophistication, there was a discernible air of disenchantment creeping through the country, as more and more people seemed disillusioned at the way things have panned out. I pointed out that it was my intention to get the hell out of this thriving, dynamic and confident market economy as soon as I possibly could and that therefore the growing sense of disillusionment about the way things have panned out was of very little interest to me, and would hopefully have little bearing on my ability to secure a beach house in sunnier climes where I could while away my middle years. As he smiled at the arrogant disdain I displayed for my native country, I thought to myself that actually, my cynical disposition coupled with my twenty-odd thousand encounters with the good, the bad and the ugly of Dublin life-forms rendered me as good a candidate as any to have a go at trying to see what had happened in the last ten years or so to have us arrive at the position we now find ourselves in.

We discussed the idea for a while, thrashing out what form the book would take, and what areas it would cover. We didn't really make a whole lot of progress there, so we left it at me undertaking to lash out 5,000 words on the proposed subject matter, so as to give Gill & Macmillan a flavour of what tack I would take with the book. (More importantly, from my point of view, the 5,000-word treatment would enable us to open up discussions on a contract for the new book. This would cover the usual guff like delivery date, publication date, word count, and most critically, my royalty percentage, which I naturally felt was due a degree of revision and enlargement now that I had established a 30,000-strong franchise of avid readers, thanks to the perhaps unexpected but nonetheless undeniable success of my début effort.)

So what you're reading now is part of the initial 5,000-word submission, written as much for my benefit as your enjoyment, in that in this prologue I will endeavour to set out my stall as it were, and outline to you, and myself, what areas I intend to cover over the following pages, some with a greater degree of insight and accuracy than others. Where I make grand sweeping statements about how things are in the world according to Donal Ruane, I will – in quite a radical break with tradition – endeavour to support my position with research and evidence culled from a variety of sources, as long as access to such sources is free, quick and easy. If for whatever reason I cannot support a particular position with empirically sound evidence, I will adopt one of two positions. The first of these will entail me making up the evidence required to suit my purposes and ascribing its origins to some very obscure publication or organisation, the veracity of which I know you couldn't be bothered to check. The second would quite simply entail me strongly advising you to take my word for it.

Anyway, hopefully there won't be too much recourse to boring facts and figures to support my stance on a particular topic. I don't want the thing ending up reading like some poxy ESRI quarterly bulletin. I'll leave that kind of guff to, well, to the ESRI I suppose. Now I've no doubt that the various bulletins and reports produced by the plethora of market research companies, policy groups and advisory committees do serve a purpose of some sorts and keep any number of people off the live register, but they don't make for very stimulating reading, do they? In trying to assess where Ireland is at right now, I think it'd be much more productive to have a look at a few key areas that dominate the everyday lives of the good folk of this country. Stuff like the property thing, the drink thing, the infrastructure thing, the racism thing and the politics thing. And then try and see how they impact on the everyday lives of these good folk, and discuss whether such impacts are to be encouraged or discouraged.

The approach I hope to take in this little investigation is, admittedly, a decidedly less rigorous one than that adopted by other noted commentators on the way things are in Ireland today. Where the likes of Fintan O'Toole, in his book *After the Ball*, chose to devour loads of reports and studies et cetera and draw various conclusions from such analyses, I have plumped for the observation angle, and feel it's as valid an approach to take as any other. And, happily, this approach involves far less research, something which I find both boring and unnecessarily time-consuming, in that it more often than not merely confirms that which I already know. As I go through the few topics mentioned above, I will call on my powers of recollection to back up my sometimes unorthodox views with a few stories and anecdotes from both my life on the streets of Dublin as a former taxi driver (God it feels good to be able to say 'former' there), and occasionally, from my life in general.

Needless to say, taking a look at a few key areas of Irish life may, from time to time, involve examining a few of the people who have, rightly or wrongly, attained a certain position in these various areas. In all probability, they will not be too pleased with the light they are portrayed in, but that's their tough shit really. And anyway, it's their own greed, thirst for power and vanity that have got them where they are, so they should be well used to someone having a go at them every now and then. I may have to at times curb the enthusiasm which I can normally so easily muster up when dealing with such colourful characters as those that populate these areas of Irish life. Given the litigious nature of these people, I'm sure you can appreciate all too well that this modicum of restraint will be exercised purely in the interests of protecting my royalties from being frittered away forking out for a barrister to defend me should one of said sensitive souls launch a libel action against me.

As I mentioned in the prologue of my first book, I do have a tendency to ramble on a bit and go off on tangents here and there, always confident that I'll make my point eventually. For those of you who found that approach somewhat frustrating, I would suggest that maybe you give it another go. Those of you who enjoyed that meandering style of writing will be pleased to learn that things in that department remain unchanged.

The Drink Thing

Only in a book about modern Ireland would the necessity arise to devote an entire chapter to the demon drink. Strictly speaking, I suppose I should really have a look at a few of the other vices that go hand in hand with the drink thing, namely cigarettes and drugs, but I don't want to use a collective kind of title like the 'The Drugs Thing' just in case I get bored with them halfway through. And anyway, however much of a problem they are in Irish society, it's probably no different to anywhere else really. The drinking thing is different though – we really are in a league of our own there. I think the latest official figures put the annual consumption of alcohol in Ireland at just under 23,000 pints a year for every man, woman and child in the country. Impressive, isn't it? Obviously that figure's bullshit. I just made it up. The real figure could even be higher, I don't know. But I do know that the couple of billion euros we piss away every year on having the craic is affecting us in some pretty major ways, and will continue to do so until we become a little more disciplined in our consumption of alcohol.

Unlike other sections of this book where I felt I should

do at least a little research to support my opinions on various matters, I had no such inclination when starting this section. I didn't even think of ringing the Licenced Vintners' Association, or Guinness, or the Department of Health or anybody like that. Not because I'm unprofessional or lazy, I hasten to add. I can be both highly unprofessional and terribly lazy alright, when a particular situation calls for such qualities, but with the drink thing I felt happy enough to ramble on for a few minutes to discuss some of the broader points relating to the issue, and then recount a few of my own experiences from my days as a taxi driver when my sole function was to ferry all manner of drunks around town. And I trust that these few anecdotes will support my assertion that we are a bit out of whack with regard to our boozing and that maybe we should pay a little bit more attention to it.

Don't get me wrong now. I'm not a pioneer or anything like that. I enjoy my few beers and a smoke as much as the next man. The only downer is that I currently have no life and consequently don't get out a whole lot. When I do, however, it's always with a great sense of anticipation and expectation. I envisage a night filled with craic – maybe a bite to eat with a bottle of wine to line the old stomach and then on to one of the four or five decent pubs that are left in this town to get a good few beers into me, nice and steady, and maybe even ending up in some awful nightclub to keep the buzz going. Things rarely pan out like that though. After the meal and a few beers I'm wrecked and just want to go home to bed.

This brings me on to the first thing I want to talk about – people's actual capacity for alcohol itself. Even after all this time cruising around Dublin each weekend, every now and then I am still dumbstruck at just how much booze people can actually put away in a single session. How people's bodies cope with that level of punishment two or three times a week, week in, week out is beyond me. Going on the lash on a Friday or Saturday is one thing, but what's even further beyond me is how people do this to themselves during the week, on a Tuesday or Thursday, knowing they have to get up at seven o'clock the following morning to be at their desk for nine. That would totally freak me out. (The getting up at seven to be at a desk for nine bit I mean. Being totally hung over as well would just render it a non-starter altogether.)

Now I'm sure at some time in your life you've gone out for the night, had one too many and left something behind you. Maybe you were out for dinner with the girls and got stuck into the vino a little too enthusiastically and ended up leaving your jacket hung on the back of your chair? Or brought your mobile with you to the toilet in case you missed that all-important call and ended up leaving it there? Could happen to anyone really. But what would you think of a lad who actually lost his wife he was so pissed? Even worse, he was so reluctant to accept the reality of what had happened, he alleged that I had somehow spirited her away for some reason. I kid you not.

It was about two in the morning and I was stuck in a tailback on the quays, behind four hundred other taxis all trying to turn left on to Parliament Street to get back to the centre of the world as Dubliners see it – Dame Street. This guy stumbles out from Temple Barf on to Wellington Quay, and my own taxi being directly in his line of blurred vision, he raises his hand in an effort to attract my attention. I had already clocked him and deduced he was a messy bastard and would no doubt wreck my head were I unfortunate enough to have to bring him home. Despite the couple of hundred taxis all around me, he had decided that I was his man and ambled towards the car pointing his finger at me and smiling as though I were an old pal he hadn't seen in years.

'Story, bud?' he slurs as he pours himself into the front seat. 'Ged in fer fucks sake, wud ye?' he then says, turning round towards the back seat.

No sign of his invisible companion joining us, so I reluctantly pull out into the outside lane and ask him where he's off to.

'Whassat?'

'Where, are, you, going?' I asked again, straining to ensure my diction was as clear as possible.

'Oh. Oh, yeah. Ah … I'm off te Donnard. D'ye know it?'

I did know it, but reckoned it would be best to confirm things with him just in case I had misinterpreted his garbled instructions.

'Up Blackhorse Avenue, yeah?' I said wearily as I went through the lights at Grattan Bridge.

'S'up on Blackhorse Avenew, bud. D'ye not know it, no?' gobshite then says, choosing to ignore my previous confirmation that I did indeed know where it was, and even at this early stage of our journey together, couldn't bloody well wait to get there.

'Taut youse are s'post te know wear yis are goin'? Not much point drivin' a bleedin' taxi if ye don't know wear yer bleedin' goin, is dere?'

The tactics called for in this situation were simply acquiescence and speed.

'You're dead right,' I answered, flooring it across the new Calatrava bridge and up Blackhall Place.

'I know well I'm righ'. I'm de bleedin' kustomar. An' de kustomar's always righ',' he says between belches.

'Issen dat righ' luv?' he then says, which scared the shit out of me for a second as I thought he was talking to me. However bad it was having this drunken sap for company, the last thing I needed was for him to be a raving homosexual. Thankfully he was referring to his imaginary friend again.

'Ye not talkin' te me now, are ye not?' he asks the absent friend in the back seat, turning his head slightly in that direction.

I had got through the lights at the North Circular and was just shooting past the barracks when your man is jolted into what I suspected was an all too rare moment of clarity and sobriety. He sits bolt upright and turns around to address the person he was convinced was in the back seat.

'Whas up wit ye?' he shouts as he turns around.

There is a moment of complete silence in the car, which I narrowly avoided shattering with loud laughter.

'Wear is she?' he then asks me accusatorily, as if I had kidnapped the female companion he was convinced had joined him in the car.

'Who?' I asked by way of reply as I swung a right turn into the estate.

'Wha' ye mean "Who"?! Me bird, ye sap! Wear is she?'

'No idea. You got into the car on your own. Where abouts do you want?' I asked as I slowed down for the ramp.

'Lissen, bud. I was wit me bird wen I got ye, righ'? An' now she's nod 'ere. Now I'm askin' ye again, wear, is she?' he said angrily, sobering up to the reality of what had happened but still not wanting to accept it, and trying to convince himself that I had indeed somehow managed to smuggle his 'bird' away from the back of the car and was now holding her captive in the glove box.

'Look,' I said wearily, pulling in to the kerb to explain things to him as they now stood. 'You got into the car on your own, okay? If you thought somebody else was getting in with you, that's fair enough, but no one did, right? And I've no idea where she is. Now that'll be €7.20, please.'

Asshole stares at me for a minute before silently accepting the logic of what I said.

'Rite bud, fair 'nough. But all I'm sayin' is, dat I can't go home widout me bird. Dere'll owney be murder, d'ye know whad I mean?'

'Well, pity about you, because we're home now.'

'Swing around dere, bud. Back inte town,' he said to me.

'You want to go back into town, yeah?'

'No, I don't want te, bud I haf te,' he explained patiently to me as he rolled down the window fully to get some fresh air before lighting up a smoke. 'I can't go out wit me bird fer de nite an' den arrive back in de gaf on me tod now, can I? Wud ye cop on?'

'Right so,' I said, flicking the meter back on, the pain I had in my arse growing larger by the minute.

I tore back down Blackhorse, on to Aughrim Street, down Blackhall Place and left on to the quays, heading for Temple Barf. All the way your man was shaking his head, wondering to himself how such a travesty could have befallen him, conveniently forgetting to take account of the sixteen pints of cider he had consumed in quick succession and how they might have affected his cognitive capacity.

'I dunno … I jus' dunno,' he muttered.

I swung over the bridge, left at The Porter House and stopped outside Fitzsimon's nightclub.

'Now can't get you any closer than this,' I said, pretending to both have an idea of where his 'bird' might be, and actually give a shit as to the whereabouts of same 'bird'.

'How d'ye know she's 'round 'ere?' he asks me, searching the deepest recesses of his pockets for some money.

'Well I picked you up just there on the quays, and that was only ten minutes ago,' I lied. 'So I'm sure she's probably just there now herself trying to get a taxi. You stroll out there and catch her, pretend you got separated coming out of the boozer, yeah?' I continued, feigning concern for his welfare.

'Is dat wear ye got me, is it, yeah?' he asked, his inability to even remember where he got into my taxi in the first place not boding too well for the probability of his finding his companion amongst the swarming mass of drunken saps now spilling out of all the pubs and clubs in Temple Barf.

'It is, yeah. I'm sure she's around the corner there,' I said encouragingly as I gave him his change.

'Sound, bud, sound,' he said, his somewhat sobered-up manner markedly changed from the narky, aggressive tone he had adopted when initially questioning my knowledge of Dublin. 'Sure ye know yerself whad is like after a few gargles, man. Ye lose de run o' yerself, don't ye.'

'Or in your case, your other half.'

It took my little joke a while to register.

'Wha?' he says as he's getting out. 'Oh yeah. Her. Very good, very good. Cheers, bud.'

Before the door was fully closed I was gone, off in search of the night's next casualty.

I'm sure your man was down in Hanlon's Corner the following afternoon for a few pints and a bit of footie, and once his memory returned, he no doubt had his mates in stitches as he regaled them with the story of how his wife went missing the previous night. You often find that the day after the night before when people are talking about their great night out. They were so locked they don't recall some hilarious joke or witticism made by them or somebody else until teatime the following evening. And then of course, the fact they didn't remember it until then is even more hilarious than that which they finally remembered. This short-term memory loss thing is a bit mad, though. That which people sometimes remember later on is quite often not funny at all and also something they would definitely rather not have happened in the first place, but they were so pissed at the time that they hadn't actually got a clue what they were doing, and worse still, use their inebriated state later on as an excuse for any wrongdoing or transgression that might have occurred.

It was on Valentine's night of this year, a Saturday it was, when I found myself tearing up Mount Merrion Avenue at just after four in the morning. Going up or down, Mount Merrion Avenue is one of the last stretches of road in Dublin where it is perfectly appropriate to make consider-able progress at a rate of seventy miles an hour. A good long, wide road, comparatively few roads leading on to it, and the vast majority of its well-heeled residents tucked up safely in bed at this hour of the morning. I had just dropped a guy off at the top of Waltham Terrace, and a very civilised chap he was too, I have to say. Generous as well – gave me a fiver tip.

So there I was tearing back up the avenue to head back towards Leeson Street when I spot this chick tottering along the pavement just past The Elms apartment complex. She was totally pissed, zigzagging all over the pavement, turning around every couple of yards to see if there was a taxi around. She sees my light on and like a fool runs out into the middle of the road to flag me down, the way people do in the movies when their SUV has broken down in the middle of Utah and they spot a tanker cruising down the Interstate. Pisses me off the way people do that – there's nothing wrong with my bloody eyesight. I slow down and pass her by, pulling over to the kerb a little way up the road. She turns and runs towards the car in a most pathetic fashion, arms flapping around like she's drowning or something. I watch her approach the back door in the side mirror and laugh as she briefly disappears from view, tripping on the kerb and going flat on her arse. I compose myself as the door finally opens and her somewhat dishevelled figure slumps across the back seat.

'God, are you okay? Did you hurt yourself?' I asked politely.

'What? Oh. Oh that, no, that was nothing,' she replied casually as she tried to manoeuvre her body into an upright position, something that took her an inordinate amount of time to do, I might add. It was as if her brain had become detached from the rest of her body and was sending instructions to her rubbery limbs from an isolated base station millions of miles away.

Once vertical, she smiles sheepishly and looks around for a minute as she tries to get herself together.

'Sorry, I know this is gonna sound really stupid, but like, where am I?' she then asks me.

'Dublin,' I answer.

'Duh, I know that much. But like, where exactly in Dublin?'

'Mount Merrion Avenue, Blackrock. Where do you want to go to?'

'Home, like,' she then replied slowly, trying to figure out if I had asked her a trick question.

'And like, where like, is home exactly, like?' I asked, somewhat irritably. Time was ticking away and all the work would be mopped up pretty soon. Was betting on her living out in Shankill or somewhere totally useless like that.

'Oh, right, yeah. Sorry, sorry,' she says slowly in a soft, kind of flirtatious voice, recognising my narky tone for what it was and trying her best to keep me onside lest I toss her out of the car for annoying me.

'I'm in Rathgar. Please. Meadowbank. It's off the Bushy Park Road. Please … Thanks.'

Doing serious overtime with the politeness thing always triggers alarm bells with me. Bad news somewhere down the line. Thought she might have been priming me for the forthcoming revelation that she only had two euros to get her home. Still, Rathgar was sweet enough. Drop her off and tear down through Rathmines. Might get another fare before it's all gone.

I move off at last. Meter's been ticking away all this time, of course – that's the name of the game. I get to the lights at the top of the avenue and swing down the bus lane to hang a left up Foster's Avenue. (Another great stretch of road for a bit of early morning speeding, especially coming down, you can really crank it up.) No chit chat as yet. She appears to be deep in thought, staring dead ahead at the headrest in front of her.

'Sorry, do you have the time?' she asks me a minute later.

'Yeah, it's just twenty past four,' I answer, waiting for her to repeat it back to me in question form.

'It's twenty past four?' she asks.

'It is,' I say, smiling to myself. 'You out past your bed time?'

'What? Oh yeah … something like that,' she says, followed by a quiet 'fuck' to herself as she takes out her mobile and looks at it for a minute, trying to figure out who it was she meant to call.

'Hello? Hello? Ciara? Can you hear me? Yeah, it's me. Where're you?' she says, running her hand through her hair as if she was on a videophone and wanted to look her best.

'No, relax, I'm fine, I'm in a taxi on the way home … I don't know, somewhere in Blackrock … Yeah, with that guy, I went back to his for a while.'

At this point she lowered her voice somewhat, lest I hear the gory details of her amorous tryst with 'that guy' back in Blackrock. Thankfully she was so pissed she had no comprehension of her speaking volume and I could still hear everything.

'I know I should have, but I didn't see you when we were leaving. … Right, well I'm sorry, okay? … What? No, I thought you knew him. Is he not a friend of Mark's?'

She starts to look a bit agitated as Ciara obviously continues to give her a bollicking for slinking off with some stranger without telling her, decent mate that she is.

'Look, I said I'm sorry, okay? ... Fuck, I don't know. I can't remember. We must have got a taxi. ... What?'

As I go through the lights at Taney Cross, under the 'Golden Gate of Dundrum', she goes silent for a minute as Ciara looks for an answer to the same question that I would have liked to ask her – did she shag this complete stranger she deserted her mates to go home with?

'Em ... well, yeah like ... we did, but ...'

But nothing. Ciara wasn't having any of it either. I could almost hear her tinny voice shrieking down the phone line.

'Ciara, please, just shut up for a second will you. I feel bad enough as it is ... I know I shouldn't have, but I did and ... What? Why? Who saw me leaving with him? Lorna? Oh shit ... is she staying with you tonight? Well, tell her not to open her big mouth, will you? Please, Ciara, just tell her I'm calling you from my house, okay? That I got home ages ago. Just left him at the taxi rank or something, okay?'

A moment's silence follows as Ciara decides how to play it.

'Thanks babe, you're a star. No, he's back tomorrow night. ... No I'm not going to tell him. He'll go apeshit. ... Yeah, well it was a one-off, okay? I was off my face and I fucked up, okay? It's not gonna happen again. ... I know I should have stayed with you, Jesus. I just wasn't thinking. ...'

Might have had something to do with the fifteen alcopops she'd lashed into her, I reckoned to myself as I was going down the hill past Mount Carmel hospital. I glanced in the rear-view mirror to see what kind of state she was in. Eyes gone a bit puffy alright. Could be some tears on the way. Hoped she could hold off until she got home to the comfort of her little pink bedroom. I didn't want to get caught up in that shit.

'Okay, hon, yeah, I'll call you tomorrow after lunch. And we'll go for a walk if it's nice, yeah? Bushy Park maybe, or a movie or something. Okay, I better go, I'm nearly home. … And make sure you say that to Lorna, won't you? Just casually like. Don't want her crazy mind working overtime. Okay, babe, love you. Bye. Bye, bye.'

She puts her phone away, clears her throat and wipes her eyes a little. I say nothing of course, pretend to be absorbed in my tunes, but I steal a glance every now and then in the rear-view. She's back to the staring thing, this time blankly out the window. No doubt she's got a lot on her mind, what with having just done the dirt on her boyfriend with a complete stranger, the web of lies and deceit she will have to concoct to keep the relationship going, the associated guilt, the worry that maybe she drinks too much and has a tendency to go off the rails. And, possibly, even the notion of getting the shock of her life next month, you never know.

'Just here actually will do fine thanks,' she says a little bit sniffily.

I pull in alongside the green as requested and total the meter. We do the money thing, she keeping her head bowed slightly, pretending to be busy organising her purse as I turn to give her her change.

'Thanks. Bye now,' she says quietly, making for the door.

'No problem. Thank you,' I reply and watched her

scuttle out of the car and trot across the green, pulling her coat tightly around her as she goes.

That's something I'm sure happens all over Dublin every weekend, but all the same, it's pretty screwed up really when you think about it. Fair enough, your boyfriend's away or whatever on Valentine's night and you decide to go out with the girls for a ladies night, have a bit of craic. Only problem is that, as on every other night of the year, blokes are out there gagging to get their end away, a good many of whom are probably already involved in relationships of their own. A good few drinks too late and you realise you've done something you wish you hadn't. It's tough. But really it's tough shit at the end of the day. Bit of discipline is all it takes.

Now, I know the cops have come in for a lot of slagging lately – and I'm always pretty quick to join in myself – but if only by the law of averages, there have to be some decent ones out there who must get a complete pain in their arse doing the night shift in the city centre at the weekend, involving as it does dealing with the effects of the binge drinking culture that has evolved. Most notable amongst these effects is the growing trend where huge numbers of people feel that after getting kicked out of a nightclub and puking on the street, their night out just isn't complete without trying to smash some passer-by's head in, said anonymous individual quite often being no more than a substitute for the bouncer of the nightclub they were previously ejected from.

It's not just skangers who start or get involved in these scraps either, as a casual drive around any part of Dublin at the weekend will show you. It doesn't matter where you come from, what you do or where you drink – too much booze makes a lot of people violent, plain and simple. Look at those blue chip boys up for manslaughter for kicking that lad's head in outside the Burlington a couple of years ago. I'm not going to comment on that particular case any further, partly because some of the parties are in the process of appealing the verdicts and sentencing, but mostly because, as a result of the unprecedented level of attention the case received from all quarters of the media, the whole country knows the ins and outs of it by now.

Anyway, the point is, I was out working that night and saw all the kafuffle as I came back in from Donnybrook, and I just drove by it; nothing out of the ordinary. Same thing no doubt happening at numerous other flashpoints around town. It's got to the stage where the provision of a serious incident unit manned by armed and trained professionals will have to be one of the conditions under which planning permission for an extension to a pub or the opening of a fast food outlet is granted.

Every week the papers are full of this shit, as are the A&E wards of James's, the Mater and Tallaght hospitals. I used to do a lot of account work for the hospitals and there wasn't a night I'd go up to collect somebody or a blood sample or whatever when the place wouldn't be teeming with drunks who had got into a fight of some sort, either with a complete stranger or worse, with a good friend, lover or family member. The family ones are the ones that crack me up, to be honest with you. I mean, we all know that Dublin's gone mad and that you don't necessarily have to go looking for trouble on your night out for trouble to visit you. You can be standing at a taxi rank, queuing in a chipper, waiting for a Nite Link, or walking home and suddenly find yourself caught up in a scrap of some sort. That's the kind of town it is now. But to have that kind of shit visited upon you by a member of your own family or a close friend, or to be the one doing the visiting, that's another thing altogether. Alcohol is always hailed as a social lubricant, and rightly so to a certain degree I suppose. It helps you relax, takes the edge off and all that, but when people get too oiled up, shit happens, stuff that's been festering or brewing for ages comes to the surface, and quite often there's no going back. Not that I can see anyway.

Take last Christmas Day for instance. I was out working, driving around, doing my thing. (Sad I know, but there you go. I had previously envisaged enjoying a cosy romantic Christmas in the company of a certain, very attractive woman, but she saw things a little differently and had dumped me three weeks previously, and so once again, I was going solo for the festive season.) Anyway, there I was with the city to myself, swinging down the coast road at ninety miles an hour. Enjoying it immensely too, I have to say. If there's one day in the year when you know it's perfectly safe to break any speed limit you like and drive around completely pissed, it's Christmas Day. Not a guard in sight; principally because most of them are too pissed to drive themselves, having spent the day lashing into the bottles that all the businesses in the locality had dropped in to them as thank yous for the preceding year's vigilance. Not that I was pissed of course. Just speeding. As I approached the Howth Road junction, I saw a chap standing there with a very forlorn-looking expression on his face – on his badly cut and bloodied face, I noticed as I pulled in to check him out. He sees me stop and shuffles slowly across the road, as if he wasn't particularly pushed about getting a taxi.

'Navan,' he says to me as he slumps into the front seat.

No 'Happy Christmas'. No 'How's it going, boss?' Just 'Navan'. At last. A punter who realised that the relationship between passenger and taxi driver constituted no more than a simple A to B transfer, that small talk was both unnecessary and unwanted. Navan though. Bit of a pain in the arse, hardly going to get a punter coming back in to town. Have to work this one out. All the way up there, wasting petrol coming back empty, festive season premium, narky looking bastard for company, no chance of a gratuity. A ton should do it.

'No problem, that'll be a €100,' I say, cheerily.

Without saying a word, he takes out his wallet and hands me two fiftys. Cash in advance; even better – no haggling on arrival. I take off like a bat out of hell, partly because I knew I could without fear of endorsement, but also because I reckoned that the main reason your man was being so quiet was because of whatever melée had resulted in him receiving the nasty cut to his right cheek, his inner rage was so great he couldn't even bring himself to speak. So, handy and all as a hundred euros was for a trip I could do in half the time it would normally take, I wanted him out of the car a.s.a.p. in case he blew up again and started in on me. He was reeking of whiskey as well; obviously had a few too many small ones.

I was up past Dunshaughlin before he deigned to open his mouth. Prior to this he had been sitting rigidly in his seat, staring out the window intently as if he were keeping an eye out for someone he had told he'd collect on the side of the road and didn't want to miss them.

'Glassed me. Glassed me, de fucker did.'

Finally. Much as I was enjoying the simple A to B transfer thing and the tunes from my CD player, nosey bastard that I am, my curiosity had got the better of me and I was dying to know what had happened to him, and had spent the previous fifteen minutes or so playing out all sorts of domestic scenarios in my head to try and ascertain which would be the most plausible.

'Oh yeah? What'd he do that for?' I asked in a concerned manner, as though I know the 'he' he was referring to.

'He's alwis havin' a go at me, de wanker. Never god on wid 'im from day one. Didden even want hur te marry me in de furst place, stewpid fucker.'

The father-in-law, I'm guessing. This should be good. I'd love to have heard that speech.

'And what's his problem?' I asked, my somewhat exasperated and conspiratorial tone implying I knew your man to be a chap of the finest character and couldn't understand why any father wouldn't be pleased to welcome him into the family.

He paused for a moment to check me out. Seeming satisfied that I appeared an ordinary bloke, and glad to have somebody to tell his side of the story to, he continued.

'Went over te deir place fer de aul dinner today, yeah? De usual carry-on, everybody bein' nice, 'tendin' everytin's grand. Den afterwards, I'm out de back havin' a smoke – ackshully, boss, wud ye mind if I had a smoke?'

'Fire away,' I said quickly, not wanting him to clam up now.

'Sound. Yer a star,' he said gratefully, quickly sparking up a cigarette and rolling down the window.

'So I'm out de back like I said, havin' me smoke, tryin' te be kool about de whole ting – didden want te go down in de bleedin' first place. She's preggers like, due in Febbery. Jus wanted te have a nice quiet day on our owen. Furst Crimbo in de new gaf like, ye know?'

'Of course I do, yeah,' I said agreeably, not having the slightest comprehension of the alleged delights marriage, joint home ownership and being in the family way would bring.

'Now I'd had a few, don't get me wrong. Had te. Help me get trew de day an' all dat – it was jus de four of is. De wife's sister an' her fella wear suppost te be dere like, but den dey fucked off te de sun fer de week at de las' minit, ye know? Can't say I blame dem eider, bedder dan bein' stuck dere wit dat wanker eyeballin' ye. Wud've bin alrigh' if dey wer dere like – her fella's sound enough, bid o' crack. But jus de four of is? Jaysus, ye cud hear a pin drop. Even her ma was gettin' stuck inte de vino, her nerves wer dat shot.'

He pauses for a second and allowed himself a brief smile at the recollection.

'Anyways, den wen she's clearin' up, she starts on about de baby, great excitement and all that, so I left 'em tew it and split out de back fer me smoke. He folleys me out an' jus' stares at me like. Jus starin'. He was flutered like, lashin' inte de gargle since de mornin' probley. Den 'e starts in, sayin' shit like if I sherk me responsibilities wit de nipper he'll have me an' all dis shit?' he says, incredulously, looking at me and nodding his head, trying to elicit my support for his position.

In fairness, I have to say he was a sound bloke, and I'm sure that himself and the missus were very happy and that he'd be a good enough father when the time came. I've met enough people in my time to be able to judge people quickly and he came across as being a decent sort of skin.

'No way?' I said, letting him know whose side I was on.

'Yeah way, man. Complete toerag 'e was. Shure I'm made up aboud de little fella. Dat's not a slip o' de tongue by de way. We know it's a boy. Deadly, id is. So I tells him te fuck off once an' fer all, dat I married 'is dawter, we're boat very happy an' if 'e's not, dat's his bleedin' problem.'

'You're dead right. Fair play,' I said, definitively. I meant it too.

'So den 'e starts roarin' at me, dere in de bleedin' gardin. Takes a swing at me bud I managed te dodge it handy enough – he's a fat bastard an' all, all over de gaf 'e was. I landed one on 'im anyways, sick o' dis shit evry time we go down dere. Good one too it was. He goes on de flat of 's back. So I taut dat'd be dat, ye know? Cool de jets like, but no, he gets up an' fuckin' charges at me like a bleedin' bull, knocks me te de ground. Me gargle goes flyin', glass smashes on de patio. He grabs it an' holds it at me face, roarin' at me like a bleedin' lunatick. I was wrestlin' away, tryin' te get de fat bastard off me, taut I was gonna bleedin' burst, an' he's dere jabbin' away at me wit de glass. Nex ting I know, I'm pourin' blood, fucker'd slashed me cheek wid it. Den de two wimin wer out o' course, screamin' an' shoutin' at de pair of is. De boat of is, can ye believe dat? An' him de one dat's after slashin' me bleedin' face! I just got me coat an' split, wassen stayin' around fer anymore o' dat shite.'

'You're right too. Fuck him anyway, he sounds like an

asshole if you ask me. Just do your own thing,' I offered by way of advice as I headed along by the river towards the town.

'Too rite, brudder, I will. … No, swing a rite fer me bud. I'm up this way,' he says, pointing towards the lights at the bridge.

He rolls up the window and directs me into his estate.

'Just here'll do grand, ta. Go in here now an' wait fer her te come back up. She'll be none too pleased eider I'd say, but fuck it, whas done is done, issen dat rite?'

'You said it, yeah. Good luck with the baby and all that,' I said.

'Sound, bud, ye've enough in de ton, yeah?'

'Yeah, it's cool. All the best.'

'Rite so, good luck,' he says as he gets out of the car, 'an' a Happy Christmas to ye an' all, yeah?'

'You too,' I replied reflexively, before realising that it hadn't really been like that for him.

He half smiled, nodded his head and walked towards his empty house.

As if that wasn't a sorry enough tale of the effects of alcohol in the season of good will, I think it was the night before that, on Christmas Eve, that a lad got beaten to death in the car park of some pub in Louth. He'd just won the lotto thing they did there and was off home with a little Christmas bonus in his pocket when some disgruntled tanked-up moron set upon him in the car park and ended up killing him. For €200.

I remember when I was sixteen – in fourth year at school – this guy I used to kind of hang around with was accorded the opportunity of joining the alleged cool set on a night out at a Friday night disco well known to most southside teenagers. Knowing that I was an alcohol virgin as well, he suggested I come along with him to share in the experience. I politely declined, reckoning that, apart from the fact that his companions on the night out were all assholes, they were also all avid rugby players and I suspected most of them to be rampant homosexuals and didn't fancy getting buggered at that tender age. Anyway, off he went on his initiation ritual. He managed two pints in some pub beforehand, puked his ring up and had to go home. The ribbing he got the following Monday was only fierce and lasted until around Thursday. (By the way, my suspicions were confirmed a few years later – I know for sure that four of them are gay as.)

Now that was what seems like decades ago, back in the year nineteen hundred and eighty six; but the only thing that has changed is that sixteen years of age would now seem like a very late stage in life to be experiencing your first taste of the amber nectar. Walk past nearly any off-licence on a Friday or Saturday night and chances are you'll see a small group of underage kids hanging around outside trying to cajole successive patrons into buying them a few cans of cheap imported lager or cider so they can go off to a field somewhere and get pissed out of their heads. The people who normally end up buying the booze for them are quite often only recent graduates of such hedge schools, spurred into action maybe by a twang of nostalgia for their own youth, or by some kind of bizarre thought process which tells them that the sooner the kids get used to the consequences of binge drinking the more adequately equipped they'll be for adult Irish life.

'Knacker drinking' is not really the correct term for it either, in that it implies that the participants in this activity are from a socio-economically challenged background, but that's not the case nowadays. There are as many genuine Hilfiger-bedecked little brats from affluent south county families at this crack as there are knockoff-Hilfiger bedecked skangers from wherever else at it. The only difference is that the skangers are somewhat more visible maybe, with the rich kids having the luxury of a free house more often as their parents' hectic social lives demand they leave their budding society queen daughter in charge whilst they jet off to London for some shopping or down to Renvyle for some golf.

As I've said before, there is really no facet of the Irish drinking thing that I haven't already seen firsthand, and whilst it has got to the stage where I am now unshockable in terms of being horrified or morally appalled by anything that goes on in Dublin, there have been a couple of occasions that have given me pause for thought – one or two incidents which, had they been captured on camera, manipulatively edited and accompanied by an ultra-grave voiceover, would have been the lead item on the news.

I referred to one such incident briefly whilst wrapping up my previous book, but I'm gonna tell you about it again because it's a bit mad. I was out working and had a fare up to Crumlin from town. The chap asked me to make a pit stop in the garage near the bridge so he could get some smokes. I duly but reluctantly obliged and swung into the forecourt. Duly because he's a sound enough bloke, but reluctantly because after dark said forecourt is nearly always thronged with any number of pond life scum whiling away the night taking turns to shout racist abuse at the night shift ethnic staff for not being able to understand their coded skanger dialect whenever they go to the hatch to reluctantly pay for some crisps to accompany their cans, and smoking whatever they can get their grubby little hands on.

And there they were. Wearing only standard issue counterfeit trackies despite the freezing cold, with baseball caps pulled low lest they be recognised by someone they didn't want to be recognised by. Genuine Nike trainers though – whatever about anything else, if you couldn't afford €100 for a pair of runners you really were poor.

Your man gets out of the car, and as with every other person who happens by, the kids size him up, gauging whether or not he's a safe bet for a bit of slagging. He's a local though and knows the shit they get up to, so when one of them approaches him on a mountain bike and completes an initial circling, he gives the kid a shove and tells him to piss off. He's a tough nut and the kid knows it so he backs down, much to the enjoyment of his mates who proceed to denounce him as a 'queer' for being stupid enough to allow a member of the public go about his business without being intimidated by a 13-year-old scumbag.

I was half watching all this with a jaded eye from the comfort of my warm car when I noticed a limp, lifeless looking kid sprawled out on the ground just around the corner from the shop, out of sight of the security cameras. Looked about twelve or thirteen maximum, either drunk out of his tiny mind or feeling the effects of his first ecstasy tab, or both. His mates had left him to lie there a while to recover, and as my punter queued at the hatch, one of the kids strolled over to give his comatose body a concerned kick, just to make sure he wasn't actually dead. The wannabe mugger on the mountain bike seized the opportunity to deflect attention from his own pathetic attempts to intimidate a grown-up and started another round of shouting and roaring, slagging off the little kid who couldn't hold his drink. The rest of the gang joined in and took it in turns to give him a few kicks as well, laughing at his rag doll unresponsiveness.

My guy gets back in the car and I take off on up the Crumlin Road to drop him on one of the roads behind the National Children's Hospital. Crumlin freaks me out with all its maze-like warrens of roads constructed in concentric circles around identikit greens, so I diligently return to the main road exactly the same way I went in. As I was going back towards town over the bridge at the canal I saw the skangers from the garage forecourt dragging the little comatose kid along the footpath, on their way to depositing him at the bottom of one of the stairwells in the Dolphin House complex. An older lad – possibly an older brother or friend of a brother of one of the gang – was passing by with his mate and creased up laughing at the state of the kid, before rubbing his head encouragingly and telling him that he'll be grand and well able for it soon enough. It's not as bad as it sounds though: his equally ossified parental unit no doubt found him in the stairwell as they returned home from their night in the pub and helped him up the stairs to their flat where he could share their curry chips before sleeping it off.

In 2002, an 18-year-old man was shot while walking through Crumlin. He died the following day. He was linked to the death of another man the previous year who was murdered over allegations by criminal figures that he was giving information to the Gardaí. The drug dealing gangster responsible for the murder of the 18-year-old was also behind a gun attack on another man that resulted in him being seriously injured, and is suspected of being the organiser of no less than five other shooting incidents in the city in the space of a year, after having taken over the operation of another man who was jailed for seven years for heroin dealing. This area of Dublin was also the scene of one of the most vicious gangland murders in recent years, when a 22-year-old man was stabbed 30 times. After part of his anatomy was severed, his body was dumped in a shallow grave.

What chance do the authorities and addicts alike have when they're dealing with psycho-kids like this? And even when they manage to jail the scumbags, it doesn't seem to stop the trade behind the prison walls. Mountjoy has a long-established culture, with up to a third of the inmates regularly using either heroin or cannabis. According to figures from the prison service, in the two years from April 1998 to May 2000, 166 seizures were recorded in the prison. The number of prosecutions resulting from these seizures is minuscule though, according to detectives. Prison guards privately concede that the regular flow of drugs into the prison helps 'keep the peace'.

Great old town we have really.

Now, much as it might perturb Michael McDowell, I'm going to divide my time here between 'hard' and 'soft' drugs. And rightly so, I think, because they are two totally different worlds, inhabited by two totally different types of people. Your hard drugs – heroin, crack, that sort of thing – are generally consumed by career addicts who are up shit creek unless they get themselves into Coolmine or Merchant's Quay or somewhere like that, whereas your soft drugs – hash, cocaine and various chemical compounds – are mostly used by normal, everyday types with good jobs in search of an instantaneous buzz on a Friday or Saturday night after a hard week in the office. Ironically, soft drugs are often classed as gateways to using hard drugs, but the evidence would suggest that alcohol, the consumption of which is our national sport, is actually the ultimate gateway drug. I'll do the hard drugs bit first.

The whole drugs thing kicked off in Dublin in the late 1960s, with a small number of people graduating from alcohol to stuff like cough bottles, amphetamines, LSD, magic mushrooms, cannabis and heroin. The Drug Squad was established as far back as 1969, with a clinic being set up at Jervis Street Hospital, which later became the National Drugs Treatment Centre. A couple of years later, in 1973, the Coolmine Therapeutic Community – a self-help, drug-free residential recovery programme – was established, and until the 1980s, which saw a huge surge in the availability of heroin, it was the only dedicated residential recovery programme for drug addicts in operation. Then the Department of Health set up the Health Promotion Unit and started distributing prevention literature and organising seminars. The spending cuts that followed threatened the survival of the few recovery facilities then available, despite the upsurge in drug addiction and the evolution of AIDS. This in turn led to increased local action with regular marches taking place, calling for more resources to be allocated to the escalating drugs problem. As more and more people became HIV positive, the treatment of drug addiction took second place behind an adopted policy of containment of the spread of HIV and Hepatitis B and C, and the heroin substitute, Methadone, was introduced.

It's estimated that there are now well over 10,000 people addicted to drugs in Dublin alone, and less than 100 in-patient beds available for detoxifying young people from drugs. There's a further couple of hundred drug-free/rehabilitation places available, the vast majority of which are made available by under-funded voluntary organisations. Do the maths yourself: the waiting lists are massive, and the problem shows no sign of abating.

Have you ever seen someone injecting themselves with heroin? I have, and it ain't pretty. I used to know this hooker pretty well a couple of years back. I'd give her a lift down to Baggot Street when she was starting work, back to the bridge from a punter's hotel after she'd turned a trick, or home to her tiny flat near the canal after a night's work. She was trying to quit the habit and took her methadone regularly, but given the nature of her job, it didn't take much for her to fall off the wagon every now and then. Could be a dodgy punter who got rough and gave her a smack, the social services restricting her access to her kids, or just the feeling that she was never going to get clean. Whatever, sometimes she just couldn't face going out to work without getting a hit of the real thing. I was trying to give her a hand out with a bit of encouragement and support and what have you, but all the same, I knew if I didn't go up to the flats with her to score she'd get a lift off someone else. And so on a couple of occasions, I found myself driving around the flats complex with her while she kept an eye out for the familiar faces she knew who could hook her up with a little bag of poison. Ever on the make, some of the little kids hanging around the place would act as middle man and run off to knock up the dealer and inform them of the whereabouts of their customers. The dealer would come down and brazenly conduct business in full view of all the residents, tipping the middle man a few quid before returning to his cooking operation. Giddy as a child on Christmas morning, she'd be smiling happily as we returned to her flat, urging me to put the foot down and hurry up.

One particular night, she suggested I come in as she was only going to be a few minutes and needed a lift afterwards. I said nothing and followed her in to her bedsit. Sparsely furnished place it was – whenever she was broke, she'd sell a telly or stereo or something to help pay the rent or send some money to her kids, only to replace the pawned items again when she managed to stay clean for a while and get some money together. With its girly colours, cuddly teddy and photos of smiling children laid out along the window sill, a quick glance around might suggest an innocent enough backstory. A root around under the bed and examination of the contents of the two old Jacobs biscuit tins lying there would tell a very different story though. One was for the money, which was more often empty than it was full. The other contained all her drug paraphernalia – tin foil, spoons, lighters and what have you. She gets out the tin and sets about finding a vein. The only one she could locate which was receptive to her intentions was in her foot, so off she goes and shoots up.

The ensuing sensation wasn't so much one like you'd see in Trainspoting where the user comes over all euphoric. It was more one of mere relief, followed by a sense of calm tempered with disappointment at having broken the last few days' clean stretch. Eight or so hours later, the stomach pains and lethargy would return and another hit would be needed. This one was enough to get her out of the flat and down to the canal, though.

Unfortunately, there are hundreds of people in Dublin caught up in a similar situation to hers, and there doesn't seem to be a whole lot being done about it. The few under-resourced clinics there are to help these people are, for the most part I'm sure, staffed by well-meaning people who do their best for those that come through the door. They can only help people who come in to them voluntarily though, and when heroin and other hard drugs are so widely and freely available throughout the city and country, I'm sure they are only treating a fraction of the number of those addicted. The real problem is with the supply end of things. If people can deal drugs in broad daylight without fear of recrimination from their neighbours or prosecution from the Gardaí, it would surely seem to confirm that nowhere near enough resources and personnel are being allocated to alleviate the problem.

It's no surprise that a lot of the people involved in the supply of hard drugs originate from, and operate from, underprivileged areas that are beset by any number of the problems that go hand in hand with living in a society of have-lots and have-nots. When a particular area gets to the stage where it is written off by the authorities and society in general for one reason or another, it makes it easier for those involved in criminal activities to conduct their business from there. To put it another way, how long do you think a drug dealer would be in business if he was operating from a house on Westminster Road in Foxrock?

Now on to the soft drugs. There are thousands of people out there who regularly consume drugs of some description for strictly 'recreational' purposes, as opposed to occupational purposes. Having worked most weekends for the last few years, I never had the opportunity to indulge myself on an experimental basis, but I know loads of people who have greatly enjoyed such experimentation and semi-regular usage of various psychedelic stimulants. These are educated people with good jobs, careers on an upward progression, all that sort of thing, and when the time came – normally a few months after they met a cool chick who told them to grow up – they seem to have been able to leave it all behind in a very disciplined and mature fashion. I know it's not based on methodically conducted research across a broad spectrum of society, but sod it, for my money, I do think there's a lot of sense to legalising some of the laws around this shit, open up the market to a bit of free trade and customer service, let people get what they want and know that they're getting good stuff and not something that's going to kill them.

Like the whole ecstasy thing, for example. If you're still doing E, you're a fool, really. Things have moved on from that shit, and a whole new range of innocently titled 'research chemicals' are now widely and legally available on the internet. Not here obviously. If our powers that be even knew what was happening on the international recreational drugs scene I'm sure they would be very much of the 'down with that sort of thing' attitude. But then that's what PO Boxes and FedEx are there for.

These new drugs give the same buzz as your traditional ecstasy tab, but are manufactured under laboratory conditions by reputable companies, not cooked up by some scumbag squatting in a grotty basement, so chances are you'll just get the high you demand without ending the night slumped on the dance floor shaking violently with blue shit streaming out of your eye sockets. It's not a perfect world, of course, so I'm sure at some stage in the future there will be people who *do* finish up their night slumped on the dance floor shaking violently with blue shit coming out of their eye sockets, but hopefully such incidents will not occur on the same scale as they have in the past with that messy ecstasy shit.

The new designer drug that's really taken off is 2,5-dimethoxy-4-iodophenethylamine, or 2C-I as it's called. (It's so new it hasn't even got a hip street name yet like Mitsubishis or whatever, but I'm sure if you type 2C-I into your Google search engine you'll get what you want.) This 2C-I is quite a powerful psychedelic stimulant which apparently shares the ups of MDMA (the main ingredient in ecstasy), and LSD (your bog standard late 1960s/ early 1970s California trip), but also has the benefit of being more predictable, and apparently has much less severe side-effects. For these reasons, the 'industry' are pinning their hopes on 2C-I becoming 'the next ecstasy', according to the trade magazine *Tab Times*. If you are off clubbing tonight, just remember that the recommended dose is 10 to 25 mg, which should have you buzzing for between five and eight hours.

(Incidentally, if you're a career clubber bored in your current job and looking for a new direction, maybe you should look at getting into this burgeoning new business. Apparently a gram of this 2C-I stuff is only $299 to buy on the net, plus shipping and handling, obviously. But with the strong euro, you could have a gram of this shit delivered to your door for about €350, and in London, where it's hitting the club scene in a big way, the street price is about £10 a pill, which is about €15. So you get your little package delivered to your door, do the necessary, and then retail it in 10 mg doses, yeah? Do the sums, people. You can gross €1,500 for your €350 outlay. Pay off a few gimps to do the leg work so there's no chance of you getting collared for the supply bit, and you're still quids in. Sweet or what?)

On a lighter note, a short one to finish up with. That same Christmas Day of last year, a couple of hours after I had dropped your man up to Navan, I found myself down around Parkgate Street and got these two lads in the car. One going up to Inchicore and the other one on to Ballyfermot. Both of them locked, obviously, the day that's in it and all that shite. They were alright though, no grief. I swing across the river at Bridgewater Quay and shoot up towards Inchicore to drop the first lad off. He gets out near St Michael's estate, explaining to his buddy that he hasn't a bean and that he'll fix up with him when he sees him next. The other lad laughs and waves him on, telling him not to worry about it, that he'll look after the fare.

'Go on, Jonner. Yer alrigh,' skin. Ye can get me a pint down de club one o' de nites.'

'I will o' coarse, Mick. Sound,' he says as he's levering himself upright with the aid of the doorframe. Once he's steady on his feet, he then addresses me with regard to his lack of funds.

'I know is Christmas an' all, buddy, bud I haven god a bean te give ye,' he says.

'Don't worry about it man, it's cool,' I answered.

And indeed it was cool. I had had a great day so far, made a nice few quid covering all corners of the city. Not content with that, though, he then rummages around in his pocket for a minute, pulls something out, puts it between his teeth and bites off a piece.

'Now son, dere ye go, liddle bid o' blow fer ye. Help ye wind down aftir yer nite's work. Out on a Christmas Day an' all,' he says, genuinely, handing me a little nubbin of hash.

'Decent man. Fair play to you. All the best,' I said, graciously taking his substitute gratuity.

Least a fiver's worth and all it was. Sound bloke.

Just for the sake of completeness, I'll do the smoking thing now. Smoking is very bad for you, health wise. No matter what anyone says, though, it's also very cool, and very sociable. I've no stories of aggression or stupidity where smoking was a significant contributing factor. If you smoke heavily over a long period of time, chances are you'll die. All told, it's probably not a good idea. Nuff said.

I'm not really going to bother my arse discussing the token sops McDowell has made to the electorate in recent times to try and convince them that he's cracking down on alcohol-related crime and anti-social behaviour. Like the changing of the last orders thing on a Thursday, for instance, cutting it back an hour. People will just go to the pub an hour earlier, or get a few shorts into them early on to kick-start the quest for that much sought after 'buzz', or simply drink even quicker than they did previously. It's not that the pubs are open for too long anyway, really, it's just that drinking has become such a fundamental part of our national psyche, there's sod all else to do.

Any excuse for a few pints and people are away to the pub. Down home for the weekend? Go for a few pints with the work crowd on Thursday, so. Friday and Saturday. On the beer with the gang back home. Sunday. Stay local, have a quiet couple of pints with the lads from the house. Monday. Football training, two quick pints afterwards. Tuesday. Take it handy – get a pizza and a DVD, maybe a couple of cans. Wednesday. European football on the telly – meet the boys down in The Barge for a few. Bang, then it's Thursday again – a few pints with the gang from the office. Even the weather's against us. When it's shit, as it so often is, the warm cosy pub offers shelter and succour. On the rare occasions when the sun shines, people decamp to Wicklow or Johnny Fox's or The Summit or somewhere like that, thinking that sitting outside in a beer garden somewhere they haven't been in ages is a change from their local.

And you can ignore the various campaigns run by the large drinks companies that implore all us to enjoy our drinking in a responsible manner. Like Diageo's 'Don't see a great night wasted' ad on the telly, for instance. The only reason they put out these ads in the first place is to make it *look* like they actually give a shit about excessive drinking. The reality is that they don't. Far from it. Diageo is the second largest drinks company in the world, yeah? It's also a public limited company, which means its primary aim is shareholder enrichment. That means year-on-year increases in sales, profits and dividends. The bean counters crunched the numbers and concluded that it made financial sense to shell out for the ads, airtime and posters rather than ending up in a situation where the marketplace is regulated to such a degree that it makes an impact on their bottom line. They don't miss a trick, though, these advertising boys. Your man in the ad is totally hip, cool clothes, trendy haircut and all that. So he's locked, making a fool of himself, big swing. Despite the woefully acted looks of disapproval the revellers in the pub give him, the reality is that everybody else in Dublin is at it too. Such antics are quite often the cause of much entertainment on a night out, and the source of much mirth the following day when the gang meet up for a few more pints and a bit of food. 'Johnny's gas, isn't he? Did you see the state of him last night?' 'Yeah, he's a riot, all over the place, wasn't he?' No chance of them showing you some drunken sap going home after pissing away his week's wages and beating the shit out of his missus in front of the kids. And I love the way they get the bit of brand recognition in at the end as well, don't you? All the premier Diageo brand names and logos at the bottom of the screen. Assholes.

Ditto with the smoking ban. It's a political thing, and nothing more. It has guaranteed Mickey Martin re-election next time round, seriously boosted his chances of becoming the next Fianna Fáil party leader, and should help him with the whole health service thing too. Charlie might lose a few million in excise duty as a result of fewer people starting to smoke or current smokers not being able to smoke as much as previously, but that's his tough shit. The Department of Health is still first in line every year for the big cheque, so if there are fewer people dying of smoking-related causes, Mickey will be able to apportion his billions in such a fashion as to get more bang for his buck.

So there we are. Most people in Dublin and elsewhere drink too much too quickly when they go out, there's a lot of drugs, hard and soft, being consumed by all manner of individuals, and loads of people smoke. Big bloody deal. Nobody in any position of influence gives enough of a shit to do anything about it, politicians and the general public alike, so good luck. Do what you will.

The Infrastructure Thing

Okay, the infrastructure thing. What can I say that hasn't already been said, and a lot of it by people who really know their stuff, like Frank McDonald of *The Irish Times*, who happily remains a voice of reason in a country gone completely mad. Not only do I propose to not necessarily say anything particularly new or revealing here, but I also run the risk of being proved horribly wrong in my conclusions in that I am writing this in February 2004 and the earliest you're gonna be reading it is October 2004, by which time at least the Luas should be up and running, so all our traffic problems could be eliminated. Only messing.

Okay, I'll do the Luas thing first. In 1997, when the now troubled Michael Lowry (still a TD, amazingly enough), announced the plan, its cost was put at a reasonable sounding €288 million. Now it's approaching €800 million, and of course if the bloody thing doesn't take off, Joe Public will be subsidising its operating losses for years to come. Given the escalating costs, questions have been asked of the Railway Procurement Agency (RPA), as to the nature of the cost overruns. In June of 2003, the Dáil Committee monitoring the progress of the Luas wrote to the RPA and asked for loads of juicy info on a number of issues, and do you know what they got by way of reply? A few top-line figures, no serious breakdowns of the various categories of expenditure which would enable them to have a go at making a few suggestions as to where money and time might be saved. On reflection, it's probably overly presumptuous to hope that a government committee could do such a thing in the first place, hindered as its members are by their own inability to live in the real world like the rest of us, but there you go, they were seen to be doing something, and that's all that matters.

Anyway, it's not the committee's request I'm interested in, it's the RPA's justification for their refusal to give mega-detailed breakdowns of the costings, as requested. 'Commercial sensitivity'. That's what they said. Did you ever hear such a load of shit in all your life? Commercial sensitivity, to my feeble mind, would come into play if there were two or more entities involved in the construction of the Luas and the RPA didn't want the other gang to see how they were doing things. Or if the RPA, in what would be classified as delusional at the very least, actually thought that they were good at this sort of thing and reckoned that after delivering the Luas project over budget and years behind schedule, they might have a pop at pitching for contracts to do the same kind of thing elsewhere, and therefore didn't want their competitors in the industry to see how they did things. The only reason they didn't break down the figures is because a detailed breakdown of where all the money is going would no doubt show up the RPA to be the bungling shower of amateurs that the public have long suspected them to be. And the government is totally complicit in this matter too. Tiny Brennan – who I have some degree of time for, I have to say – could walk into the RPA's offices anytime and get the bloody figures off them if he really wanted to. But the mess that they would surely reveal would reflect badly on him, and he's got enough shit to be dealing with just trying to keep the whole show on the road at the moment, and so has to resort to the old empathy thing, and ask the people to give it time, and that they will be 'proud' of the Luas when it's up and running. Relieved, yes. Proud? I don't know.

The whole thing has been such a shambles really. Cock-up after cock-up, it just makes you laugh, really. Except you shouldn't be laughing, because it's your money that's paying for all these cock-ups. We'll go through a few of them quickly.

Cock-up Number 1

The trams themselves for instance. They were rolling off the production lines at the GEC-Alsthom factory in La Rochelle France way back in 2001, for God's sake. As soon as it got underway, everybody knew the project would be running over schedule, so why didn't the RPA ring the boys in La Rochelle and tell them to hold off for a few months? I know you have to have the trams here to allow time for training and test runs and all that, but how long does that take? There won't have been a paying customer on the trams until June of this year, and seeing as how I sincerely doubt that GEC-Alsthom give credit terms of three years, this means that the trams – which cost €1 million each –

were paid for ages ago and have been sitting in a warehouse somewhere, for God knows how long. All this bungling has a direct impact on the total cost of the project, and is just a little bit too much to take in this day and age, if you ask me.

Cock-up Number 2

The extension from Sandyford out to Cherrywood. The RPA opted to go along the Ballyogan Road, straight through several sites which were marked as national monuments, even though a report commissioned by the RPA itself, from McHugh Consultants, had identified these monuments as being situated along the route preferred by the RPA. The report suggested that to avoid interfering with these sites the old Harcourt Street Railway line should be used instead. In their wisdom, the RPA chose to ignore the advice of the report. The ultimate cost of this bungling? God only knows. Pick a number. Then double it.

Cock-up Number 3

The Red Cow thing. This one makes me cry. Trains going through the busiest junction in the state. A shortfall of €10 million to build a fly-over for the Luas over the M50 means it now has to compete with thousands of cars and pass through three sets of lights. Even using the original costings of €288 million, €10 million is sod all, less than 5 per cent. How could this money not have been found somewhere? Now the 'stilts' solution is reckoned to cost about €100 million. And hold up delivery of the Tallaght line for another couple of years.

Cock-up Number 4

The ramp in Connolly Station. €30 million pissed away just like that. The RPA bought it for the purposes of locating the Luas terminus there. But the Luas will not terminate there. It will travel on to the Point Depot. In 2001, the RPA's then acting chief executive, Mr Donal Mangan, stated to the Board that installing a Luas stop on the ramp wasn't practicable if the service was going to run on down to the Point. The Board went ahead with their original plan anyway, with the result that the trams will now drive into the non-terminal before the driver gets out and goes to the other end of the tram so that he can continue his journey through the IFSC to get to the Point. If only the RPA could get the point. The installation of a terminus that may now not be used as a terminus has involved the acquisition and demolition of a ramp at Connolly Station, at a cost of €30 million. So far.

Cock-up Number 5

The pathetic publicity stunt Bertie pulled in March of 2001 when he parked one of the trams on Merrion Square for the weekend so that he could get a few photos taken. The €1 million tram was laid on 100 feet of track and Bertie got his photo in the paper. €30,000 of taxpayer's money well spent, I'm sure you'll agree.

Cock-up Number 6

The collapse of the road surface on Harcourt Street. The engineering firm responsible for doing the utility diversion work on the road, McCloskey's, said it issued five warnings to the RPA about the structural inadequacies of the cellars which were the cause of the collapse. An RPA project director, who shall remain nameless, said that 'all important communications relating to the project would have crossed my desk'. He went on to explain that the letters actually went to a senior RPA employee based in the Heuston Station site office, as if that would put the matter to rest. Was that senior employee not aware of this project director's importance and self-importance in the overall context of the project? Obviously not, or he would surely have made sure that the letters sent to him, whether by accident or by design, would have 'crossed' his desk.

Cock-up Number 7

Mr Donal Mangan, former CEO of the RPA. Drives his company car to work every day, but does no work. Reads a few books, surfs the net, does the *Irish Times* crossword. Even has time to tackle the cryptic one. Secretary and all sitting outside the office. Why? Because he claims the RPA breached his employment rights by replacing him without giving him any notice they were doing so, and consequently he whiles away the day – on full pay – doing jack shit while he waits for a court date to sort it out.

Cock-up Number 8

If you think the Luas will get you home on a Saturday night when you're pissed and can't get a taxi, think again. There are no plans to operate late night tram services. Just like the DART.

The biggest failure of the Luas though is the one that hasn't happened yet. In 1994 there were 940,000 cars on Irish roads. Just cars now – the total for all vehicles was 1.2 million, okay? By 2004, that figure had risen to 1.45 million, giving us a total vehicle population of 1.85 million. Up 50 per cent in just ten years, the result being that 96 per cent of all passenger journeys are now undertaken by car. The Luas is simply too little, too late, with most environmental and infrastructural commentators of the opinion that by the time the thing is actually up and running and you can travel from Sandyford to Stephen's Green in 22 minutes, the capacity will simply not be there for the project to make the serious impact on Dublin's traffic problems that was the whole idea behind the thing in the first place.

The really scary thing is that these morons in the RPA are going to be the ones charged with, no, not negligence, but the construction of the proposed Metro link which would link Dublin airport with the city centre, should it come to pass. The boys in the RPA did their sums and first said it would cost €4.7 billion to build. Then they said it would cost €3.4 billion. Maybe they were confused with the initial brief and thought the metro was to run from Dublin airport to Galway city centre? Was that it? No wonder they won't release detailed breakdowns of their costings. Where did they manage to save €1.3 billion so quickly? And they have the cheek to use the 'commercial sensitivity' line when it suits them! If their figures are so hastily thrown together that they can shave 30 per cent off the estimated costs of a project, I sincerely doubt that any of their competitors could be bothered to have a look at the way they do business.

As is the way with these things, it took an outsider with no vested interest in the project to show it could be done. Prof. Manuel Melis Maynar, the president of the Madrid metro, flew in to Dublin to basically tell Bertie & Co. that they were all thick, and that the thing could be built for about €1.5 billion, €2.6 billion max. And even still, that's outrageous when compared to the Madrid metro build he oversaw, which cost only €2 billion for 40 kilometres of line. Our proposed route is only 12 kilometres long, so even using the Prof's highest estimate, the cost comes in at €216 million per kilometre, compared with €50 million per kilometre for the Madrid line. It has to be said, though, most of his projected savings came from suggesting earth-shattering notions that our boys couldn't possibly have been expected to consider, like tunneling 24 hours a day and using a standardised design for all station stops along the route.

And do you remember what happened when the Prof. wrapped up his presentation to the cabinet members and asked them if they had any questions? Our glorious leader Bertie piped up with 'When can you start?'

Gas man, isn't he?

I saw a headline there the other day announcing that Seamus Brennan has finally got the go-ahead from cabinet to build the metro at last. The projected cost now stands at €2.4 billion. I'll go out on a limb here, and wager that the project will inevitably cost more than €2.4 billion, won't be operational until a few months after its revised completion date, will be the subject of numerous cock-ups and ultimately not deliver the solution the project is supposed to.

Now on to that other mammoth civil engineering project, the Dublin Port Tunnel and the whole height thing. Now I haven't actually managed to get inside the tunnel with my measuring tape so I can't give you a definitive answer. All I can do is refer you to a letter that appeared in *The Irish Times* in January 2002 which was written by Seán Wynne, the project engineer for the Port Tunnel. At least he was the project engineer back then. The new man in charge of the tunnel is the eminently more appropriately named Mr Tim Brick. (Funny the way some people end up in a job the nature of which is reflected in their name, isn't it? For instance, there's a lad down in Clonroche in Co. Wexford I pass by on my way to get my car serviced. He's in the well drilling and water treatment business, okay? Do you know what his name is? Seán Flood. Gas, isn't it?) Anyway, in the letter, Seán Wynne went to great pains to point out that, compared to international tunnel standards, the height of Dublin Port Tunnel is more than adequate, saying that 'at 4.9 metres clearance height, with an operating height restriction of 4.65 metres, the Dublin Port Tunnel is higher than the highest European tunnels where height limits apply'. He's the man building it, so you just have to hope that he's done his measurements properly.

Seán goes on to point out the clearance heights used in other European countries: Italy, 4.75m; Austria, 4.7m; Switzerland, 4.7m; Norway, 4.6m; Germany, 4.5m; and France, 4.3m to 4.75m. That sounds fair enough on the surface, but it is clear that with an operating height of 4.65 metres, many car transporters and extra-large container trucks, which require a height clearance of 5.0 metres and above, will not be able to use the tunnel. I find this a bit daft, to be honest with you. If we can build a tunnel with a height clearance of 4.9 metres, why can't we build a tunnel with a height clearance of 5.0 metres?

As logistics and distribution companies try to increase their efficiency and profitability, when it comes to renewing their fleets, they are going to turn to these new extra-large container trucks, and regardless of how few of them are on the road at the moment, they are bound to become more and more popular, and we won't be able for them. Dublin City Council are resolutely of the opinion that once the tunnel is open for business, there will be serious restrictions on when, and even if, trucks can go through the city centre, which is fair enough, that's the idea behind it, but the Dublin Port Transport Users' Group estimate that anywhere from 360 to 720 car transporters and extra-large containers will effectively be trapped in the port: they can't use the tunnel because it's not high enough, and they can't go through the city centre.

This potential problem was nipped in the bud in a typically Irish fashion: ban the trucks altogether. In May 2003, a spokesperson for Seamus Brennan, Minister for Transport, said, 'In other countries they have local deliveries by smaller trucks; some of these large trucks are terrifying and the Minister is not making any apologies. He doesn't think Ireland wants these supertrucks.' How exactly can a truck be 'terrifying'? It's not a bloody tyrannosaurus rex, for God's sake.

This kind of knee-jerk political reaction has characterised many regrettable decisions made in the past. Always looking for the quick fix instead of trying to think your way around the problem and find a workable solution. One man who did think of a solution though, and a very clever one if you ask me, was a fellow by the name of Rory O'Connor, who is not only a B.Eng., but also an ACSM if you don't mind, which means he knows his stuff. In a very concise letter to *The Irish Times*, Rory suggested that seeing as how the segmental lining (the walls), was already in place when the height debate started, and it couldn't be removed, the simplest solution was to lower the level at which the tarmacadam roadway was to be installed. And then narrow the roadway slightly so the trucks would clear the tunnel at the sides by moving the edges of the carriageway inwards by a few inches. Problem solved. Brilliant or what? And not only would this solve the height problem, it would also result in a substantial saving, both money-wise and time-wise, quite unlike some consultant's report which had suggested that amending the design to increase the height clearance was going to cost €30 bloody million. I'm quite sure nobody involved in the project paid a blind bit of notice to what the man said, but there'd be nothing new in that.

Incidentally, in Seán Wynne's letter that I mentioned above which, as I said, was published in January 2002, he finished up by saying that the tunnel was costing €450 million, and that it was being built to the highest international specifications, blah, blah, blah. Then when Seamus Brennan was giving his tuppence worth on the height debacle, in May 2003, he said the tunnel was costing €625 million. That's quite a jump in costs there, in all fairness – from €450 million to €625 million in a year and a half. They must be using the same financial modeling software as the RPA.

And now the M50 thing. Personally, I avoid it as much as possible until after seven o'clock when it functions largely as it's supposed to – as a motorway and not a single-storey car park. Apparently our M50 toll bridge is possibly the busiest in the world, on a vehicle per lane per hour basis at least, with some 1,700 vehicles per lane per hour using the bridge, compared to the 1,400 vehicles per lane per hour which use the George Washington bridge in New York, for instance. It's nothing to be proud of, obviously. It just shows up the lack of vision that characterised its initial design and construction.

What's even more pathetic about the M50 is the way the interchanges were designed. Instead of using what are known as clover-leaf interchanges like they do in nearly every other progressive society, our lot went for the boring old straightforward on-and-off ramps. When it was being planned and budgeted for it was estimated that the inclusion of clover-leaf interchanges in the design of the M50 would have cost £80 million. It was decided to leave them out and save the £80 million so that it could be pissed away on some other area of public expenditure. This incredibly short-sighted approach to infrastructural planning is now responsible for a huge amount of lost productivity every day of the week, and I'm quite sure that were somebody to study it comprehensively it would be shown to be now costing the country well in excess of £80 million every year. Just look at the Naas Road off-ramp for traffic travelling southbound on the 'motorway'. It is absolutely terrifying how much time you can waste inching your way up towards the lights at the roundabout. Even after they spent God knows how many millions constructing what is basically the longest filter lane in the country, the only thing that has improved is that at least now both lanes of the motorway itself are available to traffic continuing on southbound to the tailback in Ballinteer at the end of the motorway.

The motorway shouldn't end there now, of course. By this stage it should continue all the way out to Loughlinstown to join up with the N11, finally giving Dublin something approaching a ring road. But it doesn't, partly because the National Roads Authority (NRA) is behind schedule, but mostly because of the few idiots impeding the NRA's progress. I am referring to the Carrickmines castle gang here of course. Now, I am all for protecting our heritage and ancient monuments for future generations to visit only when they are showing their long-lost, yank cousins around the place, but it is simply not feasible to preserve every stone in the country just because it happens to be a couple of thousand years old. The Carrickmines protest has held up completion of this vitally important stretch of motorway for over a year and cost over €50 million in the process.

What really gets me is the ludicrously weak foundation the protestors' argument is based on. One argument they trotted out went something like this: a huge proportion of newly created jobs in Ireland over the last number of years have been in the tourism sector; if Carrickmines castle is allowed to be destroyed so a motorway can be allowed pass through the site we are effectively eliminating the possibility of further job creation in the tourism sector, so progress in one area will lead to a loss in another area. Give me a bloody break; I have never heard such a load of rubbish in all my life. I lived in Dundrum for many years and never heard a thing about Carrickmines castle. I don't recall it being mentioned in any history books in school as being a vital link to our Norman history. Nothing of major significance that has any resonance for the times we live in seems to have happened there, and I would be hugely skeptical of the long-term viability of any heritage/interpretative type centre being established there.

Moreover, if the courts had finally ruled in the protestors' favour, where was the money for its preservation and possible restoration going to come from? Dúchas is strapped enough as things are, trying to keep its existing portfolio maintained, and would, I'm sure, cite any number of historic houses and monuments elsewhere in the country that would merit heritage-related investment ahead of the castle. And even if by chance there were millions swilling around for the conservation of every pile of stones in the country and the place was restored as best it could be and three part-time jobs were created for students during the peak summer months to give tourists the twelve-minute informative tour of the place, how many people are going to visit it? Sod all, and that's the reality of it. These people should really conserve their energies for more worthwhile conservation battles that are bound to arise in the future, and in the meantime allow the rest of us get home from doing a real day's work that little bit earlier. God knows we've waited long enough to enjoy anything approaching an integrated modern road network.

Have you ever been to Copenhagen? I was there for a long weekend a while ago with this chick I was going out with. (She dumped me as soon as we got back to Dublin airport with one of those, 'It's not you, it's me ...' speeches, but there you go, story of my life. Had a great weekend all the same, though.) It's a very cool city; things just seem to work the way they're supposed to.

For starters, there's a direct rail link from the airport to Central Station in the city centre, and it worked like a dream – clean, modern trains arrived and departed on time. If they were even a minute late, you'd see people pacing up and down the platforms, scratching their heads trying to figure out what apocalyptic calamity had befallen the city, whereas in Dublin when a DART train is late, you just shrug you shoulders, light up another smoke and wait twenty minutes for some bullshit announcement to come over the loudspeaker. And there were bicycle lanes all over the city. Thousands of bikes too, obviously, and most of them left unlocked by their owners, No skangers wearing counterfeit hoodies trying to steal them either.

Given that I have spent the best part of five years chewing my fingernails to the quick as I battled with Dublin's woefully inadequate infrastructure on a daily and nightly basis in my taxi, what was particularly noticeable for me was the complete absence of road works in Copenhagen. Actually, I tell a lie, I did see one set of road works. My unbeknownst-to-me-but-soon-to-be-ex-girlfriend and I were walking along a street on Saturday afternoon and were stopped in our tracks at the sight of a rather large hole in the ground, suitably barricaded off and well signed. I would have taken a photo of it but I didn't have my camera with me.

So there we were, standing on the pavement like a pair of gobshites looking at these road works when a chap driving his van down the road crashed straight into the protective barrier the maintenance guys had thoughtfully erected around the area under repair. We laughed hysterically for a minute before checking to see if he was okay. He was fine, if a little dazed and confused. As was I: it was broad daylight, he wasn't blind, he had two arms, and appeared to be sober. I couldn't for the life of me figure out how he could have crashed in the first place. After much deliberation the most logical conclusion I could reach was that the van driver's reactions were momentarily paralysed by the unusual sight of the road works in question and he careered straight into them.

The exact same thing would probably happen in Dublin, but for the completely opposite reason. Picture the scene. You're driving down Harcourt Street towards the Green someday and to your complete shock and horror you discover that your path is strangely unimpeded by all manner of barriers haphazardly constructed by various utility contractors and our good friends in the Railway Procurement Agency. There is no doubt that your previously accredited ability to propel your vehicle in a safe and efficient manner would desert you and you'd end up ploughing into the railings of some Georgian building.

Another infrastructural innovation I noticed in Copenhagen that took my fancy was the way the Danish authorities treated pedestrian lights. At most busy junctions, the pedestrian lights are activated automatically, but if there are no pedestrians crossing, cars are free to turn left or right on to the road. Sounds logical enough, doesn't it? Compare this to the way things are done in Dublin. When pedestrian lights go green, they stay green, even when there are no pedestrians – which a lot of the time there aren't because the bastards are jaywalking fifty yards further up the road because they couldn't be arsed to cross at the designated point – and loads of cars are stuck waiting for the invisible pedestrians to cross the road before they make their turn. And don't give me the safety-of-pedestrians-is-paramount line; I'm well aware of that, but if a right-thinking society like that of our Scandinavian neighbours, with the headlights in their Volvos and Saabs on all the time, can accommodate the needs of pedestrians without unnecessary holdups for cars, why can't we?

Just to show you how pathetic the situation is here, I'll tell you a little story. True story and all. One evening when I was out working I was stopped at a tortuously unpredictable set of lights, those at the junction of Capel Street and Bolton Street, beside The Four Seasons pub. I had come around from the UGC cinema and on seeing the lights at the pub green in my favour, I put the foot down, as you do. Alas, they changed to red and I hit the brakes. I was just plugging in my travel kettle to brew up a cup of coffee, reckoning I may as well settle down for a bit whilst I waited the half hour or so it would take for the lights to go green again, when I noticed this chap standing on the road in front of my car flapping his arms wildly. I looked up at him and do you know what he was doing? Ranting at me for having had the temerity to stop with my front wheels over the stop line, thereby encroaching ever so slightly on the space available to him to cross the road between the white pedestrian lines! I couldn't believe it. What a sap. Now he was a big lad alright, but nothing a couple of months on the Atkins diet wouldn't sort out. And he was the *only* person crossing the road. I ignored him until such time as he got decidedly more vocal, and then I gave him the finger; again, as you do. He feigns a look of outrage and starts pointing furiously at my roof sign. Just for badness, I rolled down the window and confirmed that yes, I was free if he wanted a lift.

'No, I don't want a bloody lift, you ignorant bastard!' he roars at me. 'I am trying to draw your attention to the fact that you are breaking the law! Look where your car is stopped. Way over the line. You should have stopped back there. How am I supposed to cross the road?'

This defied belief. It really did. Such an incident at three in the morning after a long Saturday night would be par for the course, but it was only about eight o'clock on a Tuesday evening, and your man wasn't pissed at all. And the kettle had just boiled.

'Would you ever grow up, you sap!' I replied, as politely as I could under the circumstances. 'Haven't you got the whole road to yourself?'

'That's not the point. You are breaking the law!' he said, taking off Michael McDowell perfectly.

'Yeah, yeah. Piss off,' I parried with, rolling up my window so I could unpack my sandwiches in peace, suddenly exhausted by the whole incident, and slightly annoyed with myself for having entertained the moron in the first place.

The young Victor Meldrew goes purple in the face with my nonchalant dismissal of the validity of his argument and starts doing a pen-and-paper type motion. I had only a mouthful of my sandwich eaten when, wouldn't you know it, the lights went green. I sighed deeply at the inequity of it all, adjusted my seat to the upright position and took off up towards Dorset Street to continue my night's work. (It was 'mickey money' day, and the children's allowance money was being pissed away.)

Next morning I'm in bed when the mobile goes. I groggily answer it and, to my considerable surprise, discover that on the other end is no less a personage than one of the sergeants from the Carriage Office in Dublin Castle, if you don't mind. I confirm that he does indeed have the pleasure of speaking to Donal Ruane and then listen in amazement as he reads out the abridged details of a complaint made to his office by a member of the public in relation to my non-compliance with the rules of the road as laid down in the Road Traffic Act of 1961, and subsequent amendments. It's a fair cop, so I acquiesce to his request to come in for a wee chat about my behaviour.

And so, when I should have been at home horizontal on the sofa watching two DVDs whilst enjoying a Domino's pizza before I went out to work, the following afternoon I wrestle with daytime Dublin traffic and head in to see the gaffer. He escorts me upstairs in a very businesslike manner and once we're seated in his office, he whips out a file with my name on it. Were this the file that contained details of all my infractions of the rules of the road and encounters with the general public over the years, I was pleasantly surprised at how slim it was. The sergeant opens it up and reads the statement made by Mr Meldrew from the incident the Tuesday before. I confirm that it represented an anally accurate account of the events that transpired and candidly admit that I did indeed give the finger to the complainant, briefly outlining my justification for having done so. The sergeant sighs deeply for a moment and shakes his head. He then politely suggests that I refrain from such activity in the future.

'I don't want you coming in here wasting my time any more than I'm sure you don't want to be coming in here after your night's work,' he said in a friendly enough manner.

I agreed that that made a whole lot of sense and off I went home to my DVDs and pizza.

Now, is it just me, or was that Victor Meldrew chap a complete and utter moron? I mean, it would have been a different matter altogether if I had come tearing around a blind corner and screeched to a halt at the lights, narrowly avoiding killing him as he crossed the road with the full approbation of the green man, but it wasn't anything remotely like that. And had we had the Danish solution implemented at that particular junction, the whole thing never would have happened in the first place.

Another example. (Which is slightly redundant now because the situation, to the best of my knowledge, has been rectified, however long overdue such rectification was.) The traffic lights at the junction of the Glenageary Road Lower and Corrig Road out in Dún Laoghaire. Do you know them? Every weekend I would be out taxiing and could be up and down the Glenageary Road twenty times in a night. Without fail, when I was stopped at the lights, the opposing lights would go green, then give a filter for cars turning right on to the Glenageary Road, and then give a green pedestrian light. Without fail. At one, three, five o'clock in the bloody morning. Utterly pointless. At that hour of the morning, no traffic light should turn red unless a sensor detects that a vehicle is approaching from the opposite direction. And no pedestrian light should automatically go green unless there is a pedestrian present to cross the bloody road. It doesn't matter if the lights are right beside a school and parents are worried that their undisciplined little brat children won't press the button that might save their life; as far as I am aware, schools finish up at three or four in the afternoon. It's not bloody rocket science; all these lights have sensors and timers in them; all it takes is a technician to adjust the sequencing.

In fact, our civic authorities could do worse than examine and adjust accordingly the sequencing on nearly every set of traffic lights in this dump, because, as I'm sure many of you frustrated commuters out there would surely be able to attest to, most of them are completely out of whack with the demands of the cars that have to obey them. This bullshit sequencing of our traffic lights is, I am quite sure, a major contributory factor to the number of accidents on our roads. Cars at a junction are inching forward all the time, revving up to get away first, and cars approaching the junction from the opposite direction are putting the foot down to get through the inadequately timed green light, and then, bang, somebody's insurance goes through the roof.

An even more infuriating example of the high level of inanity which seems to be a job requirement for those charged with the implementation of these matters can be found up in Harold's Cross, at the first turn in to the Mount Argus estate, at the florists there just before the Inn on the Park pub. For a long time there was no set of traffic lights there to assist those coming out of the estate. If you were turning left to head down towards the canal, it was no big deal, really. You wait for a break in the traffic and away you go. Fair enough, if you were turning right – which very few cars did anyway – things were a little more stressful in that you had to be quick off the mark to get out. Whether it was the result of residential representations to Dublin City Council or just the boys in the traffic department realising that they had bought in too many traffic lights and decided to lash them up everywhere they could, I don't know, but a good while back, a set of traffic lights duly appeared. A complete disaster. First off, they just wouldn't turn green for those trying to exit the estate. You could sit there and sit there, watching numerous opportunities for safe and comfortable egress pass you by, but the bloody lights wouldn't change. And if you took one of those opportunities for safe and comfortable egress, well, then you were breaking a red light.

Anyway, again, whether it was through further resident-ial representations or unusually pro-active behaviour on the part of our civic leaders I don't know, but the sequencing was eventually changed. And things were even worse than before. Now, the bloody lights changed so fast if you blinked you'd miss them, thereby greatly frustrating the thousands of drivers travelling up and down the Lower Kimmage Road. An accident waiting to happen. And they happened. And I saw one or two of them. My own solution to the maddeningly frustrating situation was to treat the junction as if there were no traffic lights there at all, as had been the situation for years before. As long as there was nothing in my way, I turned left, right or progressed straight on as my itinerary demanded. And I will continue to do so until such time as I either accrue sufficient penalty points to render me legally unable to drive up and down the Lower Kimmage Road, or some gobshite in the council gets off his or her fat arse and adjusts the sequence appropriately.

In the interests of balance (and also to illustrate that adjusting the sequence at a particular set of lights is not only possible a mere thirty-five years after a man landed on the moon, but also improves the flow of traffic through that set of lights), I would like to mention a set of lights that have improved dramatically in recent times. The ones at the very busy junction of the Rathfarnham Road and Dodder Park Road. For years and years, it was the same deal as out in Glenageary. Green, red, filter, pedestrian. Religiously. Somebody somewhere in the council – quite possibly an employee who lived in the general Rathfarnham area and had to suffer this cretinous situation along with the rest of us – finally decided to do something about it and they changed the sequence. Now it works fine. The filter is activated when required, the pedestrian light goes when someone presses the button – the way it should be – and traffic flows through the junction a lot better than it used to.

Jesus, I cannot believe I have rabbited on about traffic light sequences for the last thousand words, but seriously, people, that's the stage things have got to in this city. If you are a driver I think you'll agree that it's a quality of life issue. You spend long enough stuck in traffic, anyway. The last thing you need are bullshit traffic light sequences that defy reason.

And all the money the goons in the council have spent putting up those Big Brother cameras all over the city?

What a load of shit. Do you really need some civil servant sitting in a control room looking at a bank of cameras that cost a couple of hundred grand and seeing the traffic backed-up on the Stillorgan dual carriageway or the Malahide Road and thinking to himself, 'Oh, look at that, a traffic jam on the Malahide Road at 8.42 am! How unusual, I better ring that nice Emma Caulfield in AA Roadwatch and tell her so she can inform the good people of Dublin.' For God's sake, it was like that yesterday, and it'll be like that tomorrow, but it mightn't be as bad as it currently is if the bloody lights were sequenced properly.

Couldn't finish up this bit without having a few words about that other menace to the Irish driver, particularly those of us unfortunate enough to live in Dublin. Ramps. Bastard ramps. Liam Fay wrote a great little piece in *The Sunday Times* there a good while back about the subject. (See? I'm not being trivial writing about such matters. If a journalist of the calibre of someone like Liam Fay sees fit to use his weekly column to discuss ramps, then why can't I give them some attention?)

Liam was talking about the installation of ramps in his estate – at a cost of €3,000 a bump if you don't mind – and how he thought the excessive use of a valid traffic-calming mechanism has now become a source of frustration for responsible, competent drivers. Residents were concerned at cars speeding through the estate and wanted to pass a motion to petition the local authority to do the necessary. For his part, Liam had never noticed cars speeding through the estate, but reckoned that to suggest as much at the meeting would be considered churlish. What he has noticed, though, were brat children wandering out in to the middle of the road while their negligent mothers chatted on the pavement about your one who was on with Joe Duffy the other day. Were some residents to suggest at the meeting that parents pay greater attention to their wandering toddlers, however, they would more than likely be dismissed as 'meddlesome busybodies'. And so the motion was carried – a victory for irresponsible parents and DC Kwik Fit alike.

I don't know what Liam's own parental status is, but I do approve of how he likened the veritable explosion of ramps that has occurred in recent times to 'parenting surrogates'. I couldn't agree more. I don't drive on the footpath and, in return, I expect pedestrians of all ages and sizes to remain off the road. Is that too much to ask? It's just that I thought that's what kerbs were there for, to delineate where the footpath ended and the road began.

As I write this section of the book, it is only beginning to register with me that come the end of March – when I'm supposed to have the bloody thing finished – I will have to make a big decision regarding my future driving status. My taxi insurance is up for renewal at the end of March and I am seriously tempted not to renew it, for reasons that would be obvious to any of you who took the time to read my first book of anecdotes which described my life behind the wheel of a Dublin taxi. I've had enough of the shit that goes with the job, and wouldn't mind having a go at trying to enjoy a somewhat more normal life.

The only problem with adopting this new regime would be that I would have to sit in the horrendous traffic that is now an integral part of Irish life, along with the rest of you, and watch my former comrades whiz up and down the bus lanes. Wasn't sure if I could handle it until I made a call to my insurance broker to see what the premium would be for private social and domestic insurance on my car. €1,000 as opposed to €5,000 for the taxi policy. That sealed it for me. I'll avoid driving during the day as much as possible and zip into the bus lanes at one minute past seven, something few people do, so entrenched are they in the mind-numbingly slow crawl that is commuting in Dublin today. And the money I save on insurance should finance at least four or five long weekends away. Might go back to Copenhagen.

A very quick one to finish up with, just to show you how good things can be with a lot of planning and a little foresight. I was in France last year for a few days at a friend's wedding, right? Flew in to Nice airport on Thursday lunchtime. Nice hassle-free baggage reclaim, and off into my rental car. My destination was the picturesque hilltop village of Saignon, a few miles up the hills beyond Apt. Approximate distance of journey? A mere 348 kilometres. Number of traffic lights I encountered on my journey? Not one. As in none. Number of ramps I had to traverse? Zero. As in two minus two.

PS: Just to update you on the whole car thing. I have this evening concluded a marathon negotiation session with a very nice chap to sell him my taxi licence, meter, printer, roof sign, CD player, and car – the lot. That's it for me and the streets of Dublin. I'm afraid you'll all have to do without my services from here on in. Can't take it anymore. Have just scrounged an old mountain bike from my mate, and am going to give the pedal power/ public transport thing a lash, and see how I get on.

The Property Thing

I bought my first property quite a few years back, can't remember when exactly, must have been 1996 or 1997, sometime around then. It was a two-bed, two-bath job, in what used to be an old distillery up in Smithfield. Keeping matters simple, the company developing the scheme decided to call it The Old Distillery. I bought mine off the plans, and at time of making my foray into the property market there were only two apartments left, both of them two-beds – one on the ground floor and one on the second floor. The one on the ground floor was actually part of the old distillery itself and had these stone walls and vaulted ceilings, like those in a cellar, yeah? Totally cool; whereas the one on the second floor was going to be a new build. I went for the one on the ground floor straight away. It was bigger than the other one too – 830 square feet – and a couple of grand cheaper as well.

Guess how much it was? No. Guess again. No. Guess again. No. Do you give up? £74,950. Doesn't sound like a lot nowadays, but I remember at the time there were incredulous gasps from all quarters. 'How much?' 'Smithfield? Where the hell is that?' 'On the Northside, yeah?' 'Are you mad? Sure, there's nothing but knackers up there. They'll have you robbed before you move in!' That kind of thing. Most of it uttered with a great deal of sincerity, I have to add, in that those doing the uttering were doing so with my best interests at heart. Not wishing to break the habit of a lifetime, I didn't listen to any of them. Except my mother; because you should always listen to your mother. She thought it was a great idea. And so I put down my two grand deposit, got myself a solicitor, signed the contract, got my mortgage from the Irish Permanent as it was then called, and waited for the big day.

And waited. And waited. It must have been at least a year later when I got a call to go in and have a look at it to do the snag list. Gagging with excitement, I tore into town, parked up the old taxi and swaggered ever so nonchalantly into the site office. I introduced myself to the foreman and told him what apartment number I was there to see. He sighed heavily as he laid down his hand of cards, raised his eyes towards the layabouts he was playing with and reluctantly looked for the keys to my apartment. Off we went, on a Fit Farm-type obstacle course, treading carefully across scaffolding planks laid casually over gaping holes and dodging around rubbish shutes hanging from the roof. The place didn't look half finished to me, but my main concern was the state of my own apartment. Finally Monasterboice Mick opens the door to my apartment and gestures for me to enter ahead of him.

(From having since logged well over a thousand hours of viewing property-related programmes in half-hour chunks on the telly – my favourite of which is Kevin McCloud's Grand Designs if you're interested – I now know that this gesture is not a mannerly one, but an integral part of the virtual *omerta* that exists amongst property people. If you walk into a space ahead of someone, it instantly feels smaller, and for someone who is seeing that space for the first time, it also ruins the put-your-own-mark-on-it vibe, in that it's considerably harder to envisage what you would do to a room when there is some smarmy git in a cheap suit and insufficiently compensating expensive shoes standing there smirking at you, or in my case Monasterboice Mick in his Bob the Builder hat, on the front of which his mother had thoughtfully written 'MICK', lest he lose it. His name wasn't Mick by the way; nor was he from Monasterboice, but that's what I'll refer to him as here – underneath that hard hat I reckon he was a sensitive soul and might take offence at my mentioning him.)

So in I go, straight down the hall and into the large living room. What a let down. It was a complete dump, nothing like what I had been led to believe it would be. The two-foot thick, cut stone walls and ancient vaulted ceiling which had been the main reasons I bought the bloody thing in the first place were all completely plaster-boarded over. It looked as if it had just been taken out of a box and thrown up any old way. I couldn't believe it. Mick fed me some bullshit about fire regulations and underpinnings for the new apartments above mine. I mused aloud about how remarkable it was that all the sales blurb had made a great fuss about the renovation of this character building in this historic quarter of Dublin and then they destroyed all the character of said building by plaster-boarding two-foot thick stone walls in the name of fire safety when the original building had already stood intact for much longer than the new build part of it was likely to. He gave me one of those 'I know, but sure I just build 'em' looks that let me know that the kettle in his skanky portacabin was just about boiled and that he would much appreciate it if I could direct my conservationist ramblings to An Taisce and let him continue the game of snap he and the sparks had been so engrossed in before my arrival.

I sloped off anyway, totally gutted. Had these cool floorboards sussed out down in Wexford and all, nice wide ones they were too, cut from old mooring posts. And a lovely bit of slate to lay between them which was going to follow the gentle curve of the partition wall separating the kitchen area from the living area. And an antique gramophone cabinet from which I previously – and with much anticipation it has to be said – envisaged myself dispensing drinks to cool chicks I had managed to lure back to my babe-magnet lair. And now all to no avail. I hated the place. I rang my guy in the estate agents and told him to sell it. Never even spent a night in the place. Before I could sell it, though, I had to buy it, so with heavy heart I completed the purchase, in the process getting screwed for another five grand in stamp duty, because it was classed as a second-hand property in that it had previously been used as a distillery four million light years ago. And I didn't get my first-time buyer's grant either, because I was buying a second-hand property, regardless of the fact that it was the first property I had bought. Is it just me or is that complete horseshit? The only good thing to come out of the whole sorry episode was that thanks to Monasterboice Mick and his pals squabbling over the admittedly complicated rules drawn up some years previously by the international governing body with responsibility for the game of snap (Mick himself having been elected head of the Irish chapter in a bitterly contested but ultimately victorious campaign) and the surge in property prices over the previous eighteen months or so, I made a nice few quid profit on the sale of my 830 square foot white box.

Apart from highlighting the frustrations involved in dealing with people who are in way over their head playing high stakes snap – and the obvious need for a dedicated help line to be established without delay – the preceding tale serves as introduction to an area which has had a huge bearing on Irish life in recent years, in that in the last ten years or so there has been no more widely observed economic barometer than house prices.

Basically, I will concern myself with two areas, property development and property ownership, having had some experience of both dealing with developers and owning a property, okay? In fairness, that's pretty much all there is to the property thing really. If you're reading this book, you're making a shit load of money developing property, or you're the current owner of a property, or somebody who aspires to own a property sometime in the future and is currently renting or living at home, or a homeless person keeping up to speed on the state of things here and now, and if you fall into the latter category, I sincerely hope your lot improves very soon, for there is no good reason why you should be there in the first place.

I'll do the development bit first.

Property development is a piece of piss, and anyone who tells you any different is either a moron or a property developer keen to dissuade you from getting in on the act yourself. Other than a dogged commitment to playing the long game, all you need is shit loads of cash and/or a friendly bank. (For the record, I have never personally encountered a friendly bank.) First, you buy up strategically located parcels of land. You then lob in your plans for a high-density scheme of apartments or duplexes. When you get your planning permission, you get on the phone to the marketing kids and tell them to book a few full-page ads in *The Irish Times* property supplement, organise a launch day in some hotel, sell out phase one, get the contracts signed and returned quickly, lodge these with your friendly bank as security for a loan to cash flow phase one of the development, do the same thing a few months later for phase two, and so on. Then buy some more land and start all over again. Any questions?

For example, late last year, a new development of apartments came on the market on Eglinton Road in Donnybrook. They were built in the back garden of a large house, Glaunsharoon, and were quite probably of the highest quality you could find anywhere in Dublin, on a par even with the top spec places you'd see in London. At the time I believe they were the most expensive new apartments per square foot in Dublin. All the same, though, the developer, Glandore House, bought the original house and garden for something like €2.5 million, developed the apartment block in the back garden and sold the 24 units – ranging in price from €800,000 for a two-bed to €1.5 million for a three-bed duplex penthouse – for a total of €24 million. Now, don't try and tell me that after allowing for development costs, professional fees and financing charges, Mr Glandore House didn't walk away with a couple of million euros profit.

And then there's the Mount St Anne's development down in Milltown. In 1995 Park Developments, headed up by Michael Cotter, bought about 18 acres of land from a religious order for a then eyebrow-raising figure of €11.5 million. The company lobbed in an application for a load of houses and apartments straight away, but was held up from developing the site for a number of years thanks to the efforts of a serious campaign mounted by the local residents' associations. Then a couple of years later, the company bought another 3.5 acre parcel of land from the religious order for just over €10 million. Imagine, €11.5 million for 18 acres, and then, thanks to the huge jump in house prices and consequently land values in the intervening few years, a much smaller site of only 3.5 acres costs practically the same amount! So ironically, the residents' plucky but ultimately doomed attempts to prevent the land being developed were actually to Mr Cotter's great benefit, in that when the sales campaign for the apartments eventually got underway, he was able to charge substantially more for the units than he would have been able to should there have been no opposition in the first place. The whole site is pretty much finished now, and the 500 or so apartments and houses there, are, it has to be said, very good quality homes – generous proportions, high spec finishes and serious kitchens. But again, it has to be said that Park Developments made an absolute killing on the place, racking up tens of millions in profits from the development.

Fair play to the boys mentioned above as well, by the

way. I don't begrudge any man making a few quid from a hard day's work, but what I can't abide at all is when the same fella comes the poor mouth later on when it suits him. For example, a charge that has often been levied against the leading property developers in recent times is the whole notion that they were only outwardly competitive and were in fact acting in some sort of cartel, deciding between themselves over lunch in Dobbin's how many houses to build and release each year for the peasants of the country to buy, and at what price these peasants would be granted the opportunity of buying their own home. This notion was, however, trenchantly countered in an article in *The Irish Times* in July 2000, by no better man than Seán Dunne, managing director of Mountbrook Homes. (Mountbrook Homes, and its various subsidiary and associated companies, is a serious player in the property market. Seán has made millions from the property game over the years, wisely getting involved at both ends of the market. For example, he is the man behind the middling quality modest homes in the Oldtown Mill development in Celbridge, at the launch of which in March of 2000 he woke to find people queuing in the mud to buy a house. At the other end of the scale, he's also responsible for Hollybrook on Brighton Road in Foxrock, where after having spent over €10 million buying a large detached house on a fine site he lashed up 43 of the most expensive apartments ever built in Dublin, with prices going to well over the million euro mark.) So there he is anyway in the interview, and what's he doing? Cribbing about the allegedly prohibitive costs of developing a site, and claiming that 90 per cent of housebuilders would be only too happy to fully develop all of their sites within the next couple of years! Give me a break.

Whatever the truth about cartels and the like, the fact is that there is a vast amount of land all over County Dublin and surrounding areas under the control of a relatively small number of property developers, and they do sit on it for long periods of time, developing it in a piecemeal fashion as it suits them best. And they're not breaking any laws doing that of course, but just don't try and cod us that it doesn't go on, blurting out a well-rehearsed mixture of disgust, disbelief, anger and possibly even hurt whenever the subject is mentioned. By way of example, do you remember that development up in Foxrock called Carrickmines Wood? Made all the papers and the evening news when it was launched because the large but otherwise fairly ordinary houses being sold cost a minimum of £1 million? Your man who built the houses, Michael Cotter of Park Developments, had owned the site – which was in fact the former estate of the McGrath Sweepstakes family – for the past fifteen bloody years. (I know I mentioned him a while back as well and don't want you to think for one minute that I'm picking on him or anything. I'm sure he's a perfectly nice chap, and obviously a very shrewd guy too. It's just that these are the examples that come to mind.) He had developed the site bit by bit over the years, wisely holding off on the best part of it until market conditions indicated the best time to knock up the houses that now sit there. The fifteen houses that made the news grossed him some £15 million alone, and there's another hundred or so apartments and houses on that part of the site, as well as 650 houses in The Park in

Cabinteely that kicked it all off in the late 1970s. Park is also just commencing work this year, 2004, on a sweet 12-acre site out by Dublin Airport that it bought nearly ten years ago for the now minuscule-sounding sum of €2.5 million. Add in the commercial end of things like Fashion City out in Ballymount, the North West Business Park out in Blanchardstown, a 50-acre bank in Carrickmines, total sales of some €111 million producing profits of over €15 million in 2002 and I think it's safe to say that the next ten generations or so of the Cotter clan need not worry themselves too much about how they are going to get by. And ditto for Seán Dunne's clan.

Other builders at the same game include the boys in Manor Park Homes, they who bought Charlie Haughey's dynastic seat Abbeville out in Kinsealy. They bought Ongar Stud out in Clonee five or six years before they decided to throw up 3,000 houses on it. And then there's Seamus Ross of Mennolly Homes who paid that gobshite Liam Lawlor €25,000 back in 1996 to confuse the postman and get the postcode of development changed so that it would be classified as being in Lucan and not the less desirable Clondalkin. He had sales in 2002 of over €150 million, racking up profits to the tune of €27 million. One more; this one cracks me up. Michael Whelan, the main man in Maplewood Homes, one of the biggest development companies in the country, bought an office block in London back in January of this year. As an investment for his kids. Cost him €230 million.

One thing you have to give some of these property boys though is, they do put their money where their mouth is. And why not, I suppose? When you have shed loads of it, why not treat yourself to a grand stately pile of your own? And why not avail of the very generous tax allowances available to you as you restore it to its former glory? Section 482 of the Taxes Consolidation Act of 1997 I believe it is. The house in question has to be approved by the Commissioners of Public Works and the Department of the Environment as having 'an intrinsic historical, horticultural, scientific, aesthetic or architectural interest'.

Once you get certified, though, it's sweet. €26,875 to repair the roof? No problem, write it off against the millions profit you're making in the property game. You're effectively getting a grant to live in considerable splendour. And let's face it, these lads could afford to buy these houses and do them up to the nines without the tax relief anyway, so they're laughing. Needless to say, a lot of the big players in the property and business world in Ireland have availed of these tax allowances and set themselves up in the luxury they feel they were destined to enjoy. And there's nowt wrong with that; the legislation is there in black and white and if they have the cash to indulge in such an undertaking, good luck to them. If you are the lucky owner of such a property, the deal is, that in return for you being able to write off associated renovation costs and a proportion of annual running costs, you must make the house available to the great unwashed to visit – for 60 days of the year, 40 of which must fall between May 1st and September 30th and include ten Saturdays or Sundays – at reasonable times and at a reasonable cost.

Well, one day, I washed and took myself off to one such house in south county Dublin with my mother. (It's actually quite hard to find a complete listing of what houses qualify for the scheme, where they are and when they are open. Obviously, the owners of the houses are delighted with such a situation, as the fewer visitors there are trooping through the house, the more they can enjoy it for themselves.) Can't tell you which house it was or who owned it in case they get thick with the following report, but you could find it if you really wanted to have a look for yourself. We get to the big gates and from the sign affixed to the granite wall note that our visit falls on the last day of the schedule drawn up by the owners. My mother, being the polite and demure woman she is, suggests that maybe we don't bother going in. With a derisory snort I rang the bell and announced our arrival, much to the consternation of the woman at the other end who reluctantly called off the hounds and let us in.

I drove up the gravel driveway and parked the car. What a view. Beautiful rolling lawns drew your gaze straight out across Dublin Bay. Madam opened the door and ushered us in, in as polite a fashion as she could manage. She then promptly relieved us of £7 each and presented us with a tattered and photocopied pamphlet which outlined the history of the house. She could have done worse than read the bloody thing herself because as the all-too-quick tour progressed, the gaps in her knowledge of the history of her own home were all too apparent. As I sighed disapprovingly my mother shot me a scornful look. Maybe she was right, and the busy season had taken its toll on the poor woman, and we had just caught her on a bad day? Yeah right. Narky cow didn't want us in her house at all, looked on us as nothing more than a frightfully

inconsiderate interruption to her supervision of the helps'
preparation of high tea.

Not more than twenty minutes later we were back out on
the gravel driveway, grand tour complete. Wholly
disappointing it was too. You can't help being annoyed
when you have just paid £7 each to listen to someone with
a serious information deficit try to remember the history
behind the ornate panelling and cornices of the library in
their historic home, especially when there is a tangerine-
coloured Apple Mac and assorted hardware strewn about
the place. So anyway, that was my visit to one of Ireland's
great houses, the loving restoration and ongoing
maintenance of which you have helped subsidise. Why not
try one out for yourself and see how you fare? Maybe you'll
have a great time, be warmly received, informatively
entertained and come away with a renewed interest in the
need for the restoration of our historic houses. There are
something like 134 owner-occupiers out there who have
been granted Section 482 relief on their stately piles, so God
knows, there must be a few decent sods amongst them who
enjoy showing people around their homes; they can't all be
complete assholes like that bitch.

Try Ballyorney House in Enniskerry, Co. Wicklow,
owned by Mark Kavanagh of Hardwicke Ltd, a serious
property magnate, developer of the first phase of the IFSC,
and that huge office development that stretches from Hatch
Street onto Adelaide Road, and part owner of the Four
Seasons Hotel in Ballsbridge, via his membership of the
festively named Nollaig Partnership. You must call in
advance to make an appointment to view the house and
gardens, but leave the dog at home as they are not allowed

on the grounds. Keep your children supervised at all times, and don't even think about bringing a picnic to enjoy in the shade of a majestic oak tree as that kind of thing is not tolerated under any circumstances, and numerous hounds will possibly be dispatched to savage you from limb to limb. (Don't expect to bump into Mark either. He tends to spend most of his time in Florida nowadays, what with all the kafuffle surrounding the revelation that he gave £100,000 to none other than Charlie Haughey back in 1989, £75,000 of which never actually made it all the way to the party bank account.)

Only a stone's throw from Mark's place is Charleville, beside Powerscourt Gardens, seat of the Rohan dynasty, currently presided over by one Ken Rohan, yet another serious player in the property development game. Interesting chap is Ken. He's involved in every aspect of the property game, and obviously doing very well out of it, because this place is serious, and once again, the impeccable restoration and ongoing maintenance of his fabulous pile has been subsidised by your good self, and for which assistance I'm sure Ken is very grateful. Fabulous art collection too, I believe.

I have only recently learned that this tax relief also applies to buildings used for commercial purposes. For instance, do you know that Noel O'Callaghan fella? Another property magnate: filthy rich, obviously. He has a few hotels around town, and one in Gibraltar as well, I hear, which is handy. Anyway, two of his Dublin hotels qualify for the historic house tax relief thing. Some bloke called Edward Carson was born in number 4 Harcourt Street, which now forms part of the Stephen's Green Hotel. Apparently he was a big shot in Ulster Unionism sometime and so the building was listed for heritage purposes. And what is now the Davenport Hotel was once called Merrion Hall – designed in 1863 by one Alfred G Jones – and the structure was listed as being of significant architectural merit. So when it came to throwing a hotel into these places Noel could write off various costs relating to the reinstatement of the facades etc. against the future income received from room rentals and bar receipts and what have you.

It's funny, though, the way a fella can have an intimate knowledge of certain aspects of heritage-related legislation that are to his financial advantage, and at the same time, be blissfully ignorant of other aspects of heritage-related legislation that impose certain pesky and costly obligations on him. For it is the same Noel O'Callaghan who demolished a listed building which formed part of a site he was developing on the corner of Fenian Street, near Holles Street maternity hospital. The funky looking art deco Archer's Garage – a List 1 building – got in the way of Noel's grand design for the site, so he promptly knocked it down. Over a quiet June bank holiday weekend, no less, when he probably thought all the planners and conservationists were on the piss in Galway. Did he think nobody would notice anything different on the Tuesday morning? Of course he pleaded ignorance of its listed status and narrowly avoided a fine of €1.27 million and/or two years in prison by promising hand on heart that he would faithfully reinstate the building.

A funny one to finish up with. Belgrave Square in Monkstown, Co. Dublin. The 2.5-acre gardens that form the square around which the posh houses were originally built came up for sale back in 1998. The residents of the square, justifiably anxious to preserve their square as it had been since the 1860s, submitted a tender for the gardens, but their bid was topped by Navan-based builder Eugene O'Connor. He subsequently dispatched a team of excavation contractors to the square where they began taking some soil samples and what have you. Needless to say, the genteel residents of the square nearly soiled themselves at the sight of such goings on and decided to get their arse in gear to scupper any grand plans Eugene might have had in mind for the redevelopment of the square. He couldn't have thrown up houses on it or anything like that obviously, as it was zoned for what is termed 'open space/amenity use'. He could, however, have lobbed in an application for a cemetery, or a car-park, or an incinerator or something like that, and it was this nightmare scenario that got the residents into top gear. Over afternoon tea with little nice things from Caviston's, the Belgrave Square Residents' Association agreed to set up a 'digger-watch' if you don't mind, drawing up a rota involving some 42 households in the square and a further 50 in the locality. A couple of weeks of huffing and puffing like this followed, with the plucky residents out in their Barbour jackets all day preventing the contractors from doing their job. Now, I don't know if Eugene got sick and tired of the eco warriors' efforts to thwart his development plans or if he even had any real development plans for the square at all, but I do know that after much toing and froing, the residents eventually ended up buying the square back off Eugene, netting him a handy few quid for basically doing jack shit.

Right, that's pretty much the development thing done; if I keep going I could end up in court. We'll move on to the ownership bit now, which is a much more difficult thing to analyse.

A few stats are unavoidable in this section – if only to reassure my editor that I did actually do some research for this book – and on the face of it, they actually seem to kind of fly in the face of a lot of the anecdotal evidence you hear about the Irish property market and the effect its crazy upward spiral of the last few years has had on the people of this country, but there you go. Anyway, stats are just stats, and they are purely quantitative, not qualitative, and it's the qualitative side of things that's more important because it's this side of things that can give you an insight into how things might pan out in the near future.

So. There's a thing called the Irish National Survey of Housing Quality, and it's undertaken every ten years. The figures I got my hands on – covering the period 2001 to 2002 – show that the figure for national home ownership in Ireland now stands at 82 per cent. Mad, isn't it? And, more than half of these home-owners, 45 per cent to be precise, own their homes outright; no monthly direct debit at all. The other 37 per cent are under mortgage, with the owners in the process of purchasing them. This survey also reports that only 5 per cent of those paying a mortgage in Ireland are allocating more than one third of their household income to the servicing of the mortgage. (This one third figure has generally been accepted as the level at which borrowings related to total income are at a manageable level.) Among more recent buyers, though, 10 per cent of people are spending more than a third of their total household income on the mortgage, which would seem to support the notion that new buyers are so stretched to afford their new home that they are topping up their mortgage with a term loan or something like that, and also that maybe the financial institutions are lending more than they should to certain buyers. The survey also showed that more than a quarter of those renting properties said they were spending more than a third of their income on rent, which would surely reflect the commonly agreed notion that, in the absence of any kind of rent controls in this country, most landlords are screwing their tenants around big time.

A few more stats – this time taken from a quarterly report compiled by the Department of the Environment – just to try and throw a bit more light on the situation. Out of a total of 80,000 odd mortgages advanced nationally in 2003, the average was apparently around €155,000, with the average price of a new home nationally being just over the €200,000 mark, and over €300,000 in Dublin. This still means that people up and down the country have to find at least €50,000 to get their hands on an entry level house. Where are they getting it from?

An interesting thing that these figures show is that the average loan to value ratio – the percentage of the house price that is financed by a mortgage – is falling. This implies that people trading up from an existing property to another, more superior property are more active in the market than those buying their first home, which would seem to strongly support the anecdotal evidence that there are many more young people out there *trying* to buy their first home than there are those *actually* buying their first home.

Almost €13 billion was lent to people in Ireland last year to buy residential property. Sounds like a lot of cash, and it is. Mortgage debt now stands at €55 billion, and other debts stand at €10 billion, giving us a total for household debt of €65 billion, which is definitely a lot of cash, actually being about 92 per cent of total household disposable income. Nobody seems too worried about this. I would be, firstly because the corresponding figure for the UK is 110 per cent, and we've seen at close quarters what happened there when the property thing overheated; and secondly because the 8 per cent of our disposable income we don't spend servicing debt doesn't seem – to me at any rate – to leave a lot of room for manoeuvre should things get tight and interest rates go back up to double figures, like they were what seems like four hundred years ago, but in actuality was just a relatively short fifteen or so years ago.

In 2002 the average mortgage advanced was €136,000, and as was stated above, in 2003 it was €155,000. That's an increase of about 15 per cent in twelve months, fairly significant if you ask me, which admittedly nobody has, but there you go. And yet it is generally accepted by all the economist boffins that the national level of affordability is cool enough, and that there's not a whole lot to worry about, which would seem to reinforce that 5 per cent figure mentioned above.

Now, I know all that still doesn't explain *why* people are buying all these bloody houses, but nonetheless, there's some pretty comprehensive research there, I think you'll agree. Who said stats were boring?

Anyway; now we'll go on to some of the anecdotal or

qualitative stuff, which as I said a few minutes ago, is really the heart of the matter, in my opinion.

It doesn't really happen to any great extent nowadays – which is hopefully indicative of an element of rationality creeping back into the minds of the nation's homebuyers – but why, a few short years ago, did people get out of bed at five in the morning and queue up in the dark to buy an overpriced apartment in Dublin? Or even camp out for a weekend, as has happened in a number of cases.

You know The Green Building down in Temple Barf? When it was launched in September 1994 a three-bedroom penthouse measuring 883 square feet was priced at £120,000. (Today, it would probably fetch in excess of €700,000. Even allowing for the ten-year interval, that's still a pretty mad increase. Has your salary increased by anything like 400 per cent in the last ten years? Didn't think so. If by chance it has, I'd be very interested to know where you work and if there are currently any vacancies.) People queued up to buy apartments in this allegedly cutting-edge, environmentally friendly building, equipped as it was with solar panels, retractable roof, ultra high levels of insulation, and a bike park. The ecstatic buyers all got themselves on the telly and in the papers and probably thought they were only great, but their eagerness to get their hands on the properties had set a dangerous precedent. The property market was beginning to take off again in a big way and the developers realised that if they snapped up a few sites in the middle of town in locations most people would only know as mugging blackspots and got their architects to copy the design of some trendy buildings in London and then told the marketing kids to come up with a cool, oh-sofashionable identity for the development, there would be no shortage of takers for them. And they were right. People queued up in their thousands to buy into the whole urban living thing.

(Actually, now that I think about it, the blame for the mess that is Temple Barf probably lies at the door of whatever tosser creative director came up with the idea for that ad for The Halifax years ago. Remember the one with that bloke in his loft apartment? There he was, chilling on a Sunday morning with his newspapers and muffins or whatever and his cat scampering playfully around the place, being careful not to knock over any of his tasteful home accessories, all of which were bought for little or nothing at the local flea market. Because that's what you do when you do the urban thing and live in the city centre. You go to the flea market and you chat to the locals and maybe buy a few trinkets, then stop off in some family-owned general store to stock up on provisions, go on home to your authentic loft apartment, brew up some fair trade decaf and chill out by the window with the newspaper. There's no flea market in Temple Barf, by the way. There was supposed to be one alright, it was clearly marked on the original plans for the area, and was supposed to be on Fleet Street, beside the Oliver St John Gogarty. But then, after some quiet deliberations, it was decided that a multi-storey car park would be of much greater benefit to the local community.)

In the past, some developers have even had the cheek to suggest that the fact that people had queued up to buy properties in their developments was a testament of sorts to the quality and value they were offering the purchaser.

What a load of shit. The main reason the vast majority of people were queuing overnight and longer was that they were sick and tired of having to second-guess the market's movements, and had finally decided to take the plunge and get their first property under their belt. They knew they were paying more than the property was really worth, but reckoned it was better to bite the bullet and get in before another bumper autumn season saw their capacity to repay afford them a less desirable property than the previous year.

So the queuing thing is one effect of our national obsession with home ownership, but what then is the cause of this obsession? The whole historical thing of being under the jackboot of the evil oppressor across the water for eight hundred odd years is obviously part of the reason, but there has to be more to it than that. Everybody is totally obsessed with property ownership here. In the last seven or eight years, there has been no more widely observed economic barometer than the stupefying year-on-year increases in the price of property nationwide, and particularly in Dublin. I mean, it wasn't that long ago that if you were out for a few drinks with your mates and started talking about the pros and cons of fixed or variable rate mortgages, chances are you would have been punched in the face and told to go home because you were a boring shite. Nowadays, however, if you go into some supposedly-trendy-but-in-actuality-shit pub in town on a Thursday night that's exactly what every second tosser in there is talking about. Or how they're going to leverage the massive equity in their first house to buy an apartment to rent it out, or that they've just bought a front line, two-bed in Puerto Banus.

I mean, the property thing here is so out of whack with

our European counterparts, it even served as the inspiration for an artwork completed a while ago by Swiss artists Beat Klein and Hendrikje Khune. The pair arrived in Ireland to take up a four-month studio residency at the Irish Museum of Modern Art, and after scratching their heads for a while trying to think of what to do to justify their sixteen-week holiday they hit upon the idea of creating a miniature city, using photos from the property section of *The Irish Times* to create their cityscape. (I saw it one day when I was down there and it looked quite cool, but only for a few minutes, to be honest. Is it art? as the age-old question goes. In all fairness, the resulting work wasn't really anything that a group of eight-year-olds couldn't put together after watching that cute chick on *Blue Peter* go at it with some scissors and glue and a few cornflakes boxes, but there you go, it's the thought process that comes before the execution that you're supposed to buy into.)

I was reading an interview with them a while after and they were saying that the idea came to them after realising that this obsession with property ownership was apparently something uniquely Irish. According to them, even a top-of-the-range apartment back home would only merit a few lines in the classifieds, principally because it's being advertised for rent and not for sale, as a deposit of 40 per cent would be the norm in Switzerland, thereby restricting property ownership to only the wealthy middle-aged who want to put down roots somewhere. On the upside, there is apparently a long-standing history of rent control and tenant-friendly legislation in place over there, even to the extent that if the central bank drops interest rates, landlords are obliged to pass on the reduction to their tenants! I nearly choked when I read that bit. Can you imagine trying to introduce something like that here? There'd be war. Every landlord in the country would descend on Leinster House to protest in the strongest terms, blocking the place off with their Mercs and Beemers, refusing to move them until the heinous wrongdoing was righted and they were able to return to messing their tenants around as they saw fit. In fairness the two boys did say that their system wasn't without its flaws, the principal one being that the government was probably going to have to set up a hardship fund of some sort to help out elderly people who couldn't afford to pay their rent.

Things are so mad here with the ownership thing that renting a place has almost some kind of stigma attached to it. You hear people excusing their tenant status with all sorts of things, like saying they're not sure if they're going to stay here in the long term, or that they just haven't found anywhere they really loved yet, that kind of shit. This is principally because the complete lack of legislation in place to control the rental market makes those renting apartments or houses appear to be powerless, vulnerable victims where every month of rent paid is seen as another grand or so pissed away that could have been put towards a deposit to secure their own home and finally escape the rental trap.

But if long-term renting is good enough for the people of mainland Europe, why is it not good enough for us? Or to put that another way, maybe, why are our close neighbours not too pushed about home ownership? (Now, seeing as how I don't know enough continentals personally, I can't support what I'm about to say next with factual, impartially gathered, empirical evidence, so this is one of those situations where you're just going to have to take my word for it.) They're only too happy to rent a place for years and years and not give a second thought to property ownership until they are in their mid-forties or so, if at all. Obviously, the knowledge that you are renting in a fairly legislated environment with rent controls and that kind of thing would be a comfort factor, but I reckon that the ownership thing just isn't part of their psyche the way it obviously is with us.

Maybe they kind of enjoy the fact that they aren't tied down financially to any one particular geographic spot and for that reason can comfortably explore the notion of living in another city or country for a long period of time. That's nothing an Irish person couldn't do as well, really, it's just that our mainland European neighbours seem to look upon a broader horizon than we do when considering their life options. I know that nowadays Irish people are to be found living and working in all corners of the world, but that in itself is, I would suggest, a direct result of our fairly recent accession to the European Union which enriched the country no end, got us all an education and brought the world a little closer. Maybe Irish people are just home birds? I don't know.

More importantly, I wouldn't mind if the property we were talking about was cheap, but it's not. It's totally out of whack with every other country in Europe. Unless of course you're reading some bullshit quarterly bulletin prepared by the economic research arm of some estate agents which will go to great lengths, I'm sure, to point out all sorts of reasons why the residential property market in Ireland is still a great place to put your hard-earned cash. All the same, though, the next time you see an advertisement for an ex-council house in Drimnagh which may take your fancy, stop and think for a minute. The house may very well have been renovated and tastefully updated, and now boasts lovely mock-Georgian plastic windows, indoor plumbing and half scale garden gnomes, but €340,000? I don't think so. Before you put down your deposit and organise a survey, have a quick look at what €340,000 will buy you in mainland Europe. Make you think, so it would.

So not only is the price of property in Ireland totally disproportionate to mainland Europe, our attitude to property ownership also seems to be at odds with that of our neighbours on the continent. Why is this? Are we getting something they don't get? Not really: apart from the fairly minimal benefit of the mortgage interest relief measure afforded to home-owners (which is to some degree offset by the rent relief afforded to those renting) and the recently scrapped first-time buyer's grant – which in all fairness was only £3,000 anyway – there aren't any major state-provided incentives for people to get into the property market here that don't exist in some form or other in mainland Europe, so it's not like it's significantly easier for someone to buy a house in Ireland than it is in Britain or France or Germany. However, what they do have in a lot of European countries that we don't have here is a regulated renting environment, with legislation giving tenants recourse to protective measures if their landlord is messing them around, stringently enforced rent controls capping the annual increases in rent a landlord may impose and stuff like that. Good stuff. And maybe that's it, maybe that is why we're all so mad keen to buy a house here: because whilst there mightn't necessarily be any mega direct financial incentives in place to encourage us to get into the property market, maybe a big reason for so many of us wanting to is that apart from the obvious feeling of personal comfort and security it gives us, it also allows us escape the totally unregulated renting scene, and we would rather take our chances with the ups and downs of the property market and potential interest rate rises than be a long-term victim of some asshole landlord who can, in the current environment, pretty much do as he wants.

So what've we got? House price inflation has gone mad in the last seven or eight years, developers, by and large, are complete and utter wankers, lots of people have queued up overnight to pay serious money for a house, there's billions being advanced every year in mortgages, nobody's saving a whole lot of money for a rainy day, the economists think everything's fine, and given the choice, most people in Ireland would rather risk getting themselves into severe financial straits in order to own their own home than rent one, viewing their inability to become a home-owner as a fundamental failure in the context of their personal development. Fair enough?

And now, a few words on the affordable housing initiative, something which has been the subject of much debate over the last few years. A measure was introduced in the Planning and Development Act 2000 which required developers to set aside 20 per cent of the units on their sites for social and affordable housing. (Just to differentiate, social housing is housing bought by local councils for those on the housing lists, and affordable housing is private housing sold at a reduced price in order to help first-time buyers, okay?) Now obviously this measure – Part V as it's called, presumably because it's Part V of the act – caused the developers a lot of sleepless nights because it would seriously affect the prices they could then charge for the remaining 80 per cent of the units, so they got together and made very strong representations to the government. And lo and behold, in 2002, environment minister Martin Cullen decided to relax the original provisions brought in by his predecessor Noel Dempsey, and decreed that a more 'practicable' solution would be to allow the property developers to either provide the affordable housing elsewhere or basically pay off the relevant planning authority by making a payment to them which would facilitate them in providing the accommodation. Now, given how stretched the planning authorities are in trying to provide social and affordable housing and how buoyant the top end of the housing market is, it's not hard to see what option the boys would go for. And all this after the original requirement had actually been upheld by the Supreme Court two years previously and used to good effect by some of the county councils in their efforts to provide low-cost housing to those in need of it. Handy the way things work out sometimes, isn't it?

To give you an example, Galway-based O'Malley Construction bought a one-acre site at number 20 Shrewsbury Road for a staggering €9.14 million in November 1999. This gem of a site was the location of the Chester Beatty library which had moved into new premises in Dublin Castle, and naturally enough the O'Malley boys planned to throw up a few seriously fabulous apartments on the site which would be highly desirable to Dublin high-fliers who felt their life would be complete if they could say, 'Shrewsbury Road, please' to their taxi driver as their night on the town drew to a close. They eventually got planning for seven luxury apartments, but only after lots of objections were lodged by some of the Shrewsbury Road residents. (Funnily enough, one of the objections was lodged by big-time property developer Seán Dunne. Yes, the same Seán Dunne whose disgust at suggestions that property developers were allegedly operating in a cartel-type environment I mentioned a few pages back. Small world, isn't it? You see, Seán had only recently completed the construction of a spectacular mansion on a 0.2-acre site he had paid a whopping £3 million for so, naturally enough, he was keen to ensure that nobody knocked up just any old development at the rear of his property which might detract from his enjoyment of his new pad.)

So, now with the planning secure, the only obstacle to the O'Malleys making a fortune from the sale of the apartments was the small matter of sorting out the amount of compensation to pay Dublin City Council to get out of the 20 per cent thing. And would you believe that in August 2003 it was reported that the council was prepared to accept €500,000 from the boys in lieu of providing the social and affordable housing? Sounds a bit lenient in all fairness, doesn't it? A few sums should help explain. The site cost over €9 million and planning was granted for seven apartments, right? So that gives us a site cost of about €1.28 million for each apartment. And 20 per cent of seven apartments works out at 1.4 apartments. And 1.4 multiplied by €1.28 million gives us just under €1.8 million. So that, by my reckoning, would be in and around the correct amount of compensation payable by the O'Malley boys, and not €500,000, but what do I know? What's worse, they shouldn't even be able to wriggle out of their Part V commitments in the first place, because Section 96 of the Planning and Development Act – which stipulates the circumstances under which developers can abstain from the 20 per cent thing – is normally only applicable to lands purchased *prior* to August 1999, and the lads from Galway didn't buy their Shrewsbury Road site until *November* 1999. But then, what's the point in having rules if they're not flexible?

And to finish up, I have to mention the fiasco from earlier this year when Bertie turned up with a few hundred photographers to announce the redevelopment of the old Department of Agriculture butter-testing facility at the back of Harcourt Terrace. Land around there is worth in the region of €40 million an acre, right? So this prime site, whilst less than one acre, would have a value of tens of millions if auctioned off to the private sector. You could build a lot of social housing units in a good location elsewhere with that kind of money, but no, the government decided that it would be more appropriate to build the social housing units on it instead of selling it.

In summary, what we have is a nation basically obsessed, for one reason or another, with private home ownership and loads of builders only too happy to step in and sell them the houses of their nightmares. But tempting as it is to blame the developers for the situation we're in here, we can't really because they're just doing what any profit-maximising operator would do in a rising market. And the housebuyers can't be to blame either, can they? Thousands of people all over the country simply want to put down roots somewhere, buy a house and raise a family, and hey, however much that kind of notion might freak me out, it's a totally normal impulse and there shouldn't be an excessive number of obstacles put in their way as they try to attain this quite universal goal, and if that means queuing overnight to buy a house in a new development or settling for a house in Gorey that necessitates them getting up at 5 am to drive fifty-four miles to Dublin to get to work, and they're happy enough to do that, then so be it.

So who's to blame then? Beats me, but I sure wouldn't like to be married with two kids, working hard, and trying to buy a house within an hour's drive of town.

The Racism Thing

Are you a nigger lover? I am. Didn't know I was until about two years ago when I came across one of the most reprehensible ingrates ever to have sat in my taxi, and he pronounced me as such. During those days, I quickly became accustomed to all manner of assholes ranting on about any topic you care to mention and what they'd do to sort it out, but this asshole was something special altogether.

Coming back from Ballymun one Sunday night about midnight, I was stopped at the lights at Doyle's corner. This toe rag comes shuffling over to the car and gets in. Totally pissed of course, reeking of cider and kebabs. Eventually managing to convey his destination to me, I sighed deeply and took off. He says nothing for a while, just stares at me intently, nodding his dopey head slowly in the way that sad blokes who have pissed away the last of their week's wages do. Having acted the hard man down the boozer with his hanger-on 'mates' all day, he was now dreading going home to get an earful from the wife – she being the type who actually gave a shit about putting food on the table for the rest of the week – and was trying to suss me out to see if I was 'one of his kind'. Halfway up the Navan Road another taxi, manned by a black guy, stopped for a punter just ahead of us.

'Fuckin' wankers, de lod o' dem ...' he slurs, as we pass by.

'Fuckin' niggers. Wankers, aren't dey?' he then says to me directly, articulating the subject of his vitriol somewhat more specifically, however pathetically.

'Why do you say that?' I replied, partly for something to say in the hope of quelling the drunken paranoia and consequent disposition for aggressiveness it brings on, but mostly to convey to him that I didn't share his opinion on the matter.

'Wha' d'ye mean, why do I says dat?' he said confusingly, my refusal to instantly acquiesce to his assertion making me out to be – in his mind at any rate – someone in possession of only the most basic motor neuron capabilities.

'Takin' money out o' *your* pockit, 'e is, de durty black bastard,' he continued, expanding on his position by trotting out one of the most pathetic lines of reasoning I have ever heard.

'He's not taking anything out of my pocket. I have a fare,' I replied.

'Yeah, but ye know whad I'm sayin'. Dem wankers comin' over here, takin' ower jobs, it's nod on, ye know whad I mean?' he expounded.

'No, I don't know what you mean. Have you got a job?' I asked.

'Course I've god a bleedin' job, ye sap!' he said, seemingly angry I didn't recognise him from the business pages of the papers.

'Good for you. You've got a job, and I've got a job, so what's the problem with that lad having a job?' I reasoned.

Your man was sitting up straight now, and had rolled down the window. He lit a cigarette to calm himself down a bit, so exasperated was he at my inability to grasp what he saw as the fundamental logic to his argument.

'Are yew a bender?' he then says to me. 'Is dad it? Yer a bleedin' bender an' ye'd luv a big black cock up yer hole, issen dad it?'

This bizarre quantum leap in his argument led me to believe that it was actually he who doubted his sexual orientation, kind of like your man in *American Beauty*.

'I'm not, no,' I answered. 'Are you?' I then ventured, knowing the response it would provoke.

'Ged a fuckin' grip man, coarse I'm not bent, ye stewpid prick. Fuckin' hate queers I do, durty bastards de lod o' dem!' he blurted out, nearly purple with rage.

After taking a minute to calm down, he continued with his reasoning.

'Fair enough, ye say yer nod a bender, an' I believe ye, righ'? It's jus' dat de queers love the niggers. Big fuckin' langers on dem an' all dat, ye know?' he explained. 'So tell me dis den, why don't ye hate dem?'

'Because I'm not an ignorant fuck like you,' I said, partly because I was about to puke on him I was so sick of his tirade, but mostly because I was just about to pull into the estate he had mentioned when I was unlucky enough to have the moron first get into my car.

'Whad ye say? Yew callin' me an ignorant fuck? Ye stewpid pox, stop de car or I'll bleedin' burst ye. Stop de fuckin' car! Now! I'm not goin' any furder wit a nigger lover like yew, no fuckin' way. Not gettin' driven te me door by a fuckin' eijit nigger lover like yew.'

I slammed on the brakes and pulled in to the kerb, fervently hoping that his neglect to fasten his seatbelt would result in him splitting his head open on the dashboard. Alas, no, he just shunted forward in his seat.

'There you go so,' I said totalling the meter, 'that'll be €9.10 please.'

(I never bother with the ten cents on a fare like that, principally because the ten cents due to me is easily foregone by a factor of at least five when you allow for the amount of time people spend drunkenly rooting around in the bowels of their pockets or purse for a ten cent coin. But not this time. I was going to extract the full amount due to me, no matter how long it took.) Gobshite reverted to the tactic adopted when fate had first cruelly inserted him into my lifeline, the nodding dopey head thing.

'That'll be €9.10, please,' I repeated a little louder, staring him straight in the eye, cautiously trying to assess the likelihood of an attack on my person, knowing that the only thing I had on my side was his near paralytic state of inebriation and the greatly slowed reflexes this would allow.

'I herd ye de furst time, alrigh'?' he said sternly, meeting my steely gaze with one of his own, before beginning the ritual trawl through every pocket for the exact amount due.

'Now, dere ye go, buddy,' he says to me in a mock-friendly tone, finally handing me the money after what seemed like seven hours but in fact had only been two of the most uncomfortable minutes of my life.

I unfurled the grubby fiver and counted the coinage,

pleasantly amazed to find that the stupid ignorant sap had indeed managed to hand over the exact amount.

'Ta,' I said curtly, nearly choking on the word, but not wanting to give him an opportunity for recrimination of any kind.

Asshole turns to locate the door handle and giving me a snide, sneering nod says, 'All de best now. Nigger lover.' He got out of the car slowly and before closing the door turned to give me one last snide look.

'Piss off, moron,' I said, taking off down the road with the door half open to get a turn in at the end of the cul-de-sac. Gobshite managed to remain upright and moved gingerly towards the low wall of a neighbour's house and proceeded to urinate on it, smiling pathetically at me as I drove past.

And so that's how I came to find out that I'm a nigger lover. And if being a nigger lover puts me firmly on the opposite side of the fence to a complete and utter fucking waste of DNA racist pig like him, then that's just fine by me. As far as saps like him go, I'm sure of a couple of things. One is that I'm sure he applies the same pathetic ideology to all people not born and bred in Dublin, not just black people. Another is that he's probably an ardent supporter of one of the top five football teams in the UK premiership, none of which would be in the position they are in without the undeniable athletic talents of the many players of various origins that comprise their squad. Another is that his children, depending on what age they are, will, either now or in the not-too-distant future, cite any number of international musical acts whose membership is comprised wholly, or in part, of people with a skin tone other than white, as being their favourites.

Whilst writing this section, I came across the findings of a study done there a while back on the whole racism thing, and it didn't make for very pleasant reading. It was carried out in June and July of 2001 on behalf of the Irish section of Amnesty International. Over 600 people from various ethnic backgrounds were asked a series of questions relating to their experience of racism in the emerald isle. Seventy-eight per cent said they had suffered racist abuse in public. Eighty per cent of them said they didn't think the government was doing enough to combat the problem. Over half said they wouldn't feel confident about reporting a racist incident to the guards, with only 14 per cent of respondents reckoning that their complaints would be taken seriously.

Possibly worst of all, only 5 per cent of them said they thought enough was being done to educate schoolchildren about racism. And that's the heart of it, really. Kids are highly impressionable and if they are unfortunate to have ignorant racist saps for parents it's highly likely that in the absence of any educational module being taught to them in school they will quickly adopt the same pathetic attitudes of their parents in their dealings with people of ethnic origins.

Amnesty shouldn't even have had to conduct this survey, but felt it had to in order to get a handle on how serious the problem was because the government have done jack shit about trying to assess the level of the problem here, never having carried out a similar survey on its own initiative. They're the gobshites who are supposed to have vision and lead the way for the rest us, demonstrating compassion and leadership. As we all know by now, such qualities are in chronically short supply amongst the majority of Irish politicians, especially those with responsibility for this particular issue, those in a position to ensure something concrete is done about it before we end up with a situation like that which exists in the UK where entire communities are ghettoised and isolated from the rest of society.

On the contrary, the 'smart' lads in the Dáil know that playing the race card works, and have used it as a cynical ploy to play on the irrational fears of ill-informed members of their constituencies. Take that Noel O'Flynn down in Cork North Central. Noel was first elected to Leinster House in 1997, getting just 4,943 first-preferences – a mere 11.23 per cent of the vote. He eventually scraped home to claim the last seat. Next time out, though, in the 2002 campaign, the bould Noelie was all over the papers after calling asylum seekers 'freeloaders and spongers'. He also made reference to incidents of 'illegality, criminality' and 'anti-social behaviour' amongst asylum seekers, 'who are illegal immigrants in Ireland and should be respecting the laws of this country while they are waiting for the applications to be dealt with'.

Two points, Noelie, if I may. First, there is any number of Corkonians engaged in 'illegality, criminality' and 'anti-social behaviour'. Why not shout about them? Second, an asylum seeker is only officially classified as an 'illegal immigrant' *after* that person's application for citizenship has been rejected. Obviously his comments were met with much tut-tutting and outright outrage from the great and the good, and O'Flynn, a true fucker, I mean a true FF-er, milked the situation for all it was worth. As the electioneering got underway he claimed to be merely articulating 'the resentment and concern at the dispersal and the large numbers concentrated in small communities'. There was much disquiet in party circles about his outburst, but after little debate, it was decided that the best course of action would be to take no course of action.

Happily for O'Flynn, things worked out well, and far from being out in the wilderness and punished by the electorate in the last election, he managed to bump up his vote to 7,387 first-preferences, landing him at the top of the poll, with a much improved share of 16.36 per cent, a 50 per cent increase on his previous campaign.

In Dublin, Mr Ivor Callely became caught up in some controversy over the same issue. After sitting it out for 13 years as a Fianna Fáil backbencher, Callely finally got the nod and was appointed junior minister at the Department of Health with special responsibility for services for older people. It's only a junior ministry, with half a car, but it's his first step up the power ladder, and God knows it's taken him a long time to get there. First elected to Dublin City Council in 1985, Ivor retained his seat at every election that followed. In 1987 he was selected to run for the Dáil in Charlie Haughey's Dublin North Central constituency, but didn't get in until the next election, in 1989.

One serious blot on his copybook was the whole Eurokabin affair. I'm not sure to what extent Ivor was involved with the company; and neither is he apparently, what with him first saying he was a director of the company and then that he wasn't. What I am sure of, though, is that Eurokabin went wallop in 1992, leaving behind it debts of £7 million (€8.9 million). Ivor's memory also failed him in connection with his involvement, or lack of involvement, in a company called Apollo Engineering, which operated from the same premises as Eurokabin in Baldoyle Industrial Estate, and shared the same telephone number as Eurokabin. Apollo Engineering also went into liquidation, but that's business I suppose – up one day and down the next. Happily for Ivor, in the midst of all the legal fallout that followed the collapse of Eurokabin, a judge accepted that Ivor believed he was not a director of the company, saying that he should not have been in court at all.

For many years Ivor was also a vocal supporter of Dublin taxi drivers, and in 1996 he managed to persuade the city council to overturn its own decision to issue a mere 200 more taxi licences. Needless to say, when the Progressive Democrats finally pushed through the deregulation thing a while back, Ivor lost a cause. He found another by giving voice to people's fears about immigration. He himself has stoutly denied any racist intent. 'I have stimulated debate and tried to steer it in a way that is appropriate,' he said in an interview. As far back as 1997, Callely publicly declared that what he called 'rogue' asylum-seekers should be 'kicked out' of the country, claiming that they were costing the exchequer too much money.

Amidst calls from many quarters for him to retract what many saw as his racist slurs, some 40 people placed a picket outside his constituency clinic. Happily for Ivor, though, as is all too often the way with these things, the furore was short-lived and dissipated when the more pressing matter of the team selection for an upcoming international friendly soccer match commanded the public's attention.

There's no denying that a sensible, level-headed and rational debate on our approach to asylum-seekers and all other aspects of immigration is needed; but what is not needed is a sap like O'Flynn deliberately using highly emotive language when discussing the issue, blatantly pandering to the racist inclinations of the electorate. There's plenty of other things to shout about – hospital waiting lists, inequality, affordable housing and things like that. But slagging niggers guarantees airtime and column inches to beat the band, and come polling day, it's a winner.

In an article entitled *The Political Currency of Racism: 1997–2002*, Bryan Fanning, a lecturer in the Department of Social Policy and Social Work at UCD, and author of the book *Racism and Social Change in the Republic of Ireland*, hits the nail on the head when discussing this kind of scare-mongering. He said that 'racism has a political currency because it proffers exceedingly simple explanations for complex social problems. For example, housing shortages or urban decline might be blamed on immigrants or ethnic minorities rather than upon, say, bad planning or inadequate funding. In such a context societal racism is a commodity with potential political value.'

When the Amnesty survey was published in September 2002, the minister with responsibility for the area, John O'Donoghue, whilst en route to South Africa to represent Ireland at the World Conference on Racism of all things, managed to make a quick pit stop in Nigeria to sign ... a deportation agreement! Great move, Johnny, really sending out the right message there. And then when he stands up to deliver his tuppence worth on the issues, he trots out some rhetoric-filled bullshit, saying it was the government's intention 'to ensure racism and racist tendencies do not gain a foothold' in Ireland. If he'd carried out a similar survey to the one Amnesty did in the first place, as he bloody well should have, he'd have realised that things were well past that stage, and that racism in Ireland is now unfortunately quite an entrenched phenomenon, and not something that we can stave off from developing in the first place.

Thankfully, at the last cabinet reshuffle, John boy was assigned to the Department of Arts, Sport and Tourism and is now back on more familiar ground, overseeing the production of crap Irish films and going to GAA matches and the like.

I know of one brilliant, multi-talented young woman of immigrant stock who cannot wait to graduate from college. So she can pack her bags and emigrate to a country that will recognise her talents first and not her skin colour. This girl got one of the best Leaving Certs in her year, including an A in honours Irish, if you don't mind. When she graduates with a likely first, she will be an asset to any community she belongs to. It won't be this one, though, thanks very much. Why? Because she is sick and tired of being called a nigger and a wog in the street by ignorant toerags who aren't fit to hold a door open for her to walk through. The many benefits of all those straight As, the honours degree in the bag and the postgraduate qualifications that will follow are going to be lost to her own country – whose native language she speaks better than the ignorant morons who hurl insults at her can speak English. Go figure.

Not surprisingly, the cops came in for a lashing in the survey's findings too, with the 622 people who took part in the survey citing 155 incidents where they had experienced racism of some form from a Garda. I know the Garda Racism and Intercultural Unit has been set up to combat these and other issues, but it's really only a sop to those who have made calls for such a unit to be established. It's woefully under-resourced and under-staffed, and will, in all probability, through no fault of its own, end up as nothing more than a purely cosmetic attempt to deal with a serious issue, because dealing with serious internal problems is definitely not the Gardaí's forte, as anyone who saw that *Prime Time* special at the start of the year would know. Scarily, race crimes reported to the Gardaí will be administered through a new module being incorporated into the Pulse computer system. Half them can't even use the bloody thing.

It's precisely because historically we're more used to people *leaving* the country in search of economic fulfilment elsewhere than we are to people coming *here* in search of economic fulfilment that we don't really have a comprehensive immigration policy in place for people whose origin is outside the EU. The main reason many of these people want to come here is purely economic, and there are basically two entry options open to them in their quest to get here.

The first option is to go through the asylum process, which many Irish people feel is now being abused. And they'd be right. It is, but principally because the absence of a proper immigration policy in the first place leaves these people with no option but to use the asylum angle as a means of getting into the country legally. And if they go down this route, they're not allowed to work here legally until their asylum application is approved, something that can take years to do because the system is woefully under-developed and under-resourced, and unlike thousands of lazy Irish bastards, these people are only too willing to work hard in low-status, low-paid jobs with minimal benefits, principally because bad and all as it might be, it's a hell of a lot better than what they could expect back home.

The second way non-EU nationals end up here is by entering the country illegally. Fraught with danger as this is, it's becoming increasingly common, and as we have seen in the past, can have tragic results. Once here, these illegal immigrants gradually merge into Irish society, getting work in many different industries that find it difficult to fill low-level jobs; and it's probably fair to say that a lot of them end up being exploited by their employers. Just look at that ex-junkie, ex-whore Samantha Hutton and the antics she got up to with her domestic cleaning agency, At Hand Cleaning Services. She had a number of Brazilian people in her employ as cleaners, and she treated them like shit, on some days making them work from 8am until 2am the following morning. The workers were driven to their various places of work in a van with blacked-out windows, for fear they got to know their way around. And once they decided to seek legal advice to see what they could do to regularise their situation, what did bitch face do? Stopped giving them work. Their plight only came to the attention of the public when they had to go to a neighbour's house begging for food and the story hit the news.

Hutton was eventually ordered to pay the three Brazilians €50,000 in compensation, but given that the company had little or no assets and was liquidated shortly after the case, it's highly unlikely the poor sods will get anything. Such judgments can often be little more than pyrrhic victories for the victims of such abuse, thanks to the ease with which irresponsible employers can liquidate a company on a Friday afternoon, buy another shelf company for a couple of hundred euros and be back in business on Monday morning. At Hands Clean Services becomes By Hand Cleaning Services in a matter of hours and the abuse starts all over again.

The Equality Authority, established in October 1999, stated that 22 per cent of all claims received in 2003 were on the grounds of race. Clearly abusive bitches like Samantha Hutton are in plentiful supply. But, thankfully, there are a good number of companies out there who actually embrace diversity in the workplace and introduce new procedures and systems that help to ensure a smooth integration into the workforce for non-national workers. Dublin Bus, for example, appointed an Equality and Diversity officer in 2000, and has also established a cultural awareness group to represent the different nationalities in its workforce, and now employs drivers from 45 different countries, such drivers accounting for 10 per cent of all its drivers.

Others that haven't followed suit had better get their act together. In 1999 the OECD estimated that there were 118,000 non-nationals living in Ireland, giving Ireland the third highest foreign population rate out of 22 European countries it surveyed, whilst the latest CSO census figures for 2002 state that there are 224,261 non-nationals living here.

Of course, being Irish, when the shoe is on the other foot and we hear of one of our mates being called Paddy in

London, or wherever, we're the first to express our horror and condemn the racist attitude of the Brits. In America recently, Satan, I mean George Bush, decided to recognise the great contribution made to the US by people working there illegally and allow them the opportunity to acquire legal status. Biffo Cowen, as Minister for Foreign Affairs, decided he had better comment on it and welcomed this magnanimous gesture on behalf of the 50,000 or so Paddys – sorry, that was racist of me, I mean people from the island of Ireland – living there, saying it was a great chance for these 'undocumented foreign workers' to regularise their situation.

Classic isn't it? An Irish person who goes to the US illegally to work is – according to Biffo, and by extension the Irish government – an 'undocumented foreign worker'. Yet somebody who arrives in Ireland from Lithuania illegally and gets a job labouring on a construction site is classified as an 'economic migrant', or even worse, as an 'undocumented alien', as if they just landed in a spaceship from bloody Mars without any identification. Even our government has the capacity to be racist, and if it can't formulate a policy of its own to deal with the problem, the least it might do is watch its language.

A t the end of the day, overcoming the racist attitudes held by so many Irish people is really only a matter of education. Don't go 'Du-uh!', as if that's totally obvious. What I mean is that there is nothing deep rooted in our history – nothing that I can think of anyway – that could possibly give us any genuine reason for holding racist attitudes towards black people. The only people we ever had a row with were the Brits, and judging by the amount of money we spend in UK-owned stores and how fervently tens of thousands of Irish people support the UK Premiership rather than the League of Ireland, we seem to have forgiven them for that couple of century's long occupation.

What's even more pathetic about the ignorant bastards who hold racist views in this country is that they seem to do so on a selective basis only. On the one hand, they'll cheer on Tiger Woods in the US Open, or rush to get tickets to see 50 Cent down in The Point, but after a few beers with their mates they'll slag off the first person they see whose skin isn't spotty and pasty like theirs. Doesn't make sense to me.

So what to do about these racist morons? The first thing to do is do your bit as a right-thinking citizen of a country with a well deserved history of being open and welcoming. One that, even in the face of this and many other obstacles, still just about has the capacity to save itself from morphing into a complete and utter shithole. This could mean doing something as simple as smiling and saying 'How's it going?' to the next non-Irish newspaper vendor you come across whilst stuck in traffic trying to make a right turn at any number of gridlocked junctions that are a by now familiar feature of commuting in Dublin. It's not going to cost you anything, and you're not going to get anything tangible out of it, but it might register with the person concerned as the friendly gesture it's intended to be.

Sounds simple, doesn't it? And it is, but if everybody did

it maybe their sense of self worth – such sense being worth just as much as yours – might gradually be elevated to a level where they don't get up in the morning already imbued with the shit feeling I can't begin to understand, where they perceive themselves as destined to being always looked upon as less than worthy of aspiring to something like the comparatively privileged life you lead.

And then, who knows? Maybe in a few years time a different climate will prevail and one day they'll be sitting there at the same junction in their own car, stuck in probably even more horrendous traffic than you were today, on their way home from a job where they are treated as nothing more than an equal by their colleagues.

Wouldn't that be cool? I think so. And if you don't, I sincerely hope that on the same day as your beautiful and intelligent daughter arrives home from studying in Paris to announce her engagement to a proud black man, that your Lotto numbers finally come up and you would have been the sole recipient of an all-time high jackpot but for the fact that you couldn't get to the shop in time because you missed fourteen sets of green lights at a notoriously busy junction where all the cars in front of you decided to buy a paper from, and exchange a few pleasantries with, a newspaper vendor who just happened to be black, and that on his arrival home his wife gleefully informs him that they have won the Lotto jackpot, on the back of a two panel quick pick she did on the spur of the moment after one of her children found a two euro coin on the footpath that afternoon as they were retuning home from her having collected them from the same school as the one your youngest child attends, said child also happening to be great friends with the newspaper vendor's children.

Remember when you were a kid and your mother took you to visit a friend's house and your friend's mother gave you some sweets? And your mother prompted you to say thank you? Manners, people. That's all it takes. Manners, and a little bit of respect. Surely we're not all gone past that?

The Tribunals Thing

Acouple of years ago I was slogging around the mean streets of Dublin, earning a living driving a taxi. I was, and still am, very interested in property of all sorts, particularly light-filled spacious contemporary homes that are well designed and well built. Given the pathetically designed nature of most of the shoeboxes that have been thrown up in Dublin over the last ten years or so, which after six months or so show signs of the wear and tear you would expect to find in twenty-year-old apartments, a cursory glance through the property section would confirm to me that no such property existed (at least not at a price that would make it attainable for a man of my means, contrary to the situation on mainland Europe). All the same, taking my cue from the Gardaí from Pearse Street, I used to make it my business to pop into the Irish Times on Fleet Street just after midnight on a Wednesday to grab a free paper and have a quick look at what was on offer.

And so it was on this particular Wednesday night. I grabbed a complimentary paper and parked up to have a quick read. A full-page ad caught my eye, and I read on with great interest. A new development called Custom

House Square was to be launched later that day. Located in the heart of the IFSC, it was one of the last Section 23 developments to have 80 per cent relief attached to it. Basically, what this meant was that purchasers could offset the rental income from said apartment – and other property they owned qualifying for similar relief – against the purchase price of the apartment itself, until 80 per cent of the initial purchase price of the apartment had been recouped in tax-free rent. Needless to say, given the reluctance of most landlords to even give their tenants a rent book, never mind pay tax on rent received, the development was bound to sell out very quickly, and I was going to have to act fast if I was to make a quick buck. I took off home, grabbed my cheque book and shot back into the IFSC where the selling agents were going to take the bookings for the apartments.

The sales office wasn't due to open until twelve noon, but when I arrived at about five am there were already a few cars parked up in front of me. I parked my piece of shit taxi behind a wine-coloured BMW seven series and formulated my master plan. The apartment I had my eye on was a south-facing one-bed on the second floor of the block, and was ludicrously priced at £175,000. The *de rigueur* parking space was a further £25,000, add another £15,000 or so for a good quality fit out, and you were looking at a cool £215,000 to get the show on the road. Just as well rents were sky high, wasn't it? Now I had no more got £215,000 to be buying an apartment in the IFSC, but I knew full well that there were plenty of people desperately trying to bury that kind of money in such an apartment. So what I had planned to do was get in there and talk the talk with the estate agents, reserve the apartment, and then get cracking on trying to pass on the contract for the actual purchase of the apartment to somebody who was in a position to complete the deal, and who, quite frankly, would have more call for it than I would.

There were plenty of people in Dublin at this crack, and it had become known as turning, appropriately enough. Very simple, really. You buy an apartment or house in a desirable development on the launch day, normally a Thursday, wait for phase one to sell out in a matter of hours and be reported in the papers the following day, and then do your damnedest to pass on the contract for sale of the property to someone else before the time came for you to actually sign the contract and go ahead with the purchase yourself. Allowing for the issue of contracts by the developer's solicitors, the standard timeframe for your response, and a few working days for understandable delays like your being in London on business for a few days or some such bullshit excuse, you would probably be looking at about three weeks maximum to pull off your little coup.

I had tried this kind of thing once or twice before, but alas, no cigar. What had stymied my success on previous occasions was actually finding someone to pass the contract on to, which was obviously fairly fundamental to the whole enterprise. Each time I put my name down for an apartment, I knew there were disappointed punters who hadn't got in on time, but I had no well-connected middle man who could act as a broker in the deal. But this time things were different. I had some months previously got to know a chap who worked for an estate agents in Dublin. This crowd had built up quite a reputation, specialising – at that time at any rate – in the sale of city centre tax incentive apartments. This lad was fairly well-connected, knew a good few wealthy businesspeople who had shed loads of cash to bury in bricks and mortar, so I was confident he could hook me up with one of them, and that they would be only too willing to compensate me handsomely for passing on the contract for my valuable tax shelter.

So there I was, sitting in my taxi, waiting for the sales office to open. Even though I had seven hours to kill, I didn't want to fall asleep in case some tosser tried to skip the queue. A couple of more cars rolled up a while later and the occupants got out and skulked around, sussing out the competition, before returning to their vehicles to sit it out with the rest of us. I decided it would be best to make a list with my fellow speculators, and approached the chap in the BMW parked in front of me. He thought this was a great idea, and declared that he was the second to arrive on site, the first being a bloke in a Jaguar parked across from us. And so it went. By mutual consent, I wrote down who was first, second, third etc. and established that my rightful position in the queue was sixth. We all chatted amongst ourselves for a while and returned to our cars safe in the knowledge that the estate agents would be only too happy to go along with our list. Anyone else who arrived thereafter was advised to make contact with me in order to safeguard their position in the by now rapidly lengthening queue.

Once I had thirty names on my list, I handed a blank sheet of paper to investor number thirty-one and told him to continue on. Shortly after, the foreman of the site, who had seen what was going on, opened the gates to the development so that we could all park up in an orderly fashion and await the arrival of the estate agents. Even though the sales office was not due to open until twelve noon, the estate agents got wind of what was happening and arrived down on site shortly after nine, laden down with muffins and orange juice. The boys in front of me declined the food and beverages, eager to politely inform them that a list had been compiled fairly and accurately and that it would be in their best interest to stick to it rigidly. I duly handed over the list and after quickly inspecting it, the estate agents sensibly decided to co-operate and issued us all with numbered tickets, telling us that we would be brought in to inspect the plans in groups of ten and that we could then place booking deposits on the apartments of our choice.

At this stage, there were swarms of people on site clamouring for position, but I didn't give a shit, mine was secure. I went up to the show apartment with my new friends and was ushered into a living room where the plans were available for inspection. The other boys were gas, they didn't even have a look around at the place, enquire about service charges, completion dates, or anything like that. The only question they asked was how many apartments they could buy, and appeared a little disappointed when told that each individual had a maximum allocation of two apartments. Time came for yours truly to do the deed and I strolled in to the living room and enquired about the availability of my previously selected apartment. It was still available, so I nabbed it, carefully pointing out that I had not yet decided whether or not I was going to complete the purchase in my own name or put it through a company and that it would be best to put 'in trust' on the title documentation so that my solicitor could amend it as necessary. Obviously, there was no such debate raging in my head – the 'in trust' insertion was merely to facilitate the hassle-free transfer of the contract to a third party at a later stage. The estate agents duly acquiesced and I handed over a cheque for £5,000, it being a refundable booking deposit.

(Now, not only did I not have £215,000 to complete the purchase of this apartment in Custom House Square, in either cash or credit terms, I didn't even have £5,000 for the deposit. What I did have though was an MBNA cheque book. My credit limit was £5,000 and I was already up to about £3,000 prior to writing the cheque. I reckoned it would be the following Tuesday or Wednesday before the cheque would hit my account so I needed to act fast or the deal was scuppered.)

And so I split home, ringing my buddy in the estate agents on the way to let him know what I had got my hands on. Suitably impressed, he confidently informed me that he could hook me up with an individual desperately in need of the tax relief attached to the property, and confirmed that such an individual would be willing to pay me a generous finders fee in return for me transferring the contracts from my solicitor's office to their solicitor's office so that they could complete the purchase. Pleased with my progress, I got some much needed sleep and waited for the phone to ring. And ring it did, and on the other end was a fellow called Tom (not his real name, for obvious reasons), who, it turned out, ran a very successful business up in Tallaght (not the real location of his business, again for obvious reasons). He told me that my buddy had given him my number and told him that I had something he might be interested in. I told him about the property and he muttered disconsolately that he had in fact – rather naïvely in my opinion – gone down to the sales office at about eleven that morning to try and get his hands on one of the apartments. Barely suppressing a smug chortle, I consoled him briefly before suggesting we meet up the following afternoon to have a look at the property and see if we could do a deal. He suggested three and I pushed it back to four, cunningly telling him that I had to meet someone else at three who was interested in it as well.

Four o'clock rolled around and I met the bould Tom in the lobby of Jurys. To look at him, you wouldn't think he had a pot to piss in, dressed as he was in boots, mucky jeans, crumpled shirt and an ill-fitting tweed jacket, but it turned out he had eight apartments dotted around the city, all rented out at exorbitant rates, some of which he had never even laid eyes on, he was that busy. The foreman let us in to the block and Tom had a quick look around, muttering approvingly about the build quality which, it has to be said, was substantially better than that which was to be found in most other developments around the city. I showed him the booking deposit form to reassure him that this prime piece of real estate, complete with an effective tax credit of about £160,000, could indeed be his if the price was right. A bit of horse trading ensued and he eventually bet me down a grand from my original asking price. Cash, of course. We shook hands on the deal and arranged to meet the following Monday to do the necessary. I rang my solicitor to keep him up to speed with developments and he agreed to do his bit in passing on the contracts to Tom's solicitor, which was a perfectly legal undertaking on his part, I must add.

I worked away all weekend, ferrying all manner of drunken saps around town, and waited patiently for Monday afternoon. Tom rings and tells me he's on the move, and I suggest we meet in the Texaco garage in Rathfarnham. I get a paper and park up, awaiting Tom's arrival with great eagerness. He pulls up in this piece of shit Renault 19 car van and I go over and hop in the passenger seat. We exchange pleasantries and then he hands me a Brown Thomas bag. I open the bag discreetly and to my great joy discover that it contains a shit load of cash. All fifties. I weighed the bag up and down in my hand for a minute, trying to give Tom the impression that I could accurately figure out how much cash was in the bag by weight alone. I quickly counted one of the wads of cash and multiplied it by the number of wads in the bag, satisfying myself that it did indeed contain the sum agreed on a few days previously, inclusive of the £5,000 I had originally put down for the deposit. I then took out my phone and rang my solicitor to let him know that all was going to plan and that he should dispatch the contracts to Tom's solicitor.

Our business concluded, I thanked Tom, shook his hand and wished him well with his new acquisition. He muttered something incoherent, I got out, returned to my car and took off like a bat out of hell. I went straight to the bank and lodged a couple of grand to my credit card account so the cheque I wrote for the deposit would clear. I then split home and locked myself in my room to count out my loot properly. There's nothing like the smell of hard cash, especially lots of it and I was delighted with myself. After hiding the cash under my bed, I went out and got completely locked. Next day, I met up with my connection from the estate agents and gave him his share of the booty. My solicitor charged me a professional fee, plus VAT, for his initial handling and subsequent forwarding on of the contracts, which was speedily and happily discharged, leaving me with a tidy enough profit for doing very, very little.

That was as close as I have ever come to being on the receiving end of one of the brown bags that are now an integral part of doing business in Ireland, particularly in relation to property matters. I must however clarify a couple of anomalies between my own little deal and the kinds of things we have been hearing about down in Dublin Castle. First off, my own bag was in fact a Brown Thomas bag. Might seem like a technicality, but hey, I'm a classy kind of guy, I just wanted to point that out. Secondly, my little transaction was perfectly legit – simply a matter of supply and demand. There was no loss to the public purse on account of my taking the initiative. If anything, the public purse was swelled somewhat as a result of my enterprising nature, in that I had to pay a bit of Capital Gains Tax on my profit, so there. (Just to put my own little deal in some kind of context, I'll give you another example of the same kind of thing, albeit on a much more attractive scale. David Arnold, a very shrewd operator, bought the old Bank of Ireland Finance office building on Burlington Road in Ballsbridge back in 1997, right? Paid £4 million for it, and within a matter of weeks he had sold on the contract for about £6.5 million to Fyffes, a full two months before he was due to complete his own purchase of the building in the first place. A £2.5 million pre-tax profit for doing jack shit. Sweet or what?)

Now I don't want you to tune out for this section. I know there have been acres of newsprint devoted to the shenanigans that seem to pass for normal business conduct these days, but in all fairness, to really have any idea of what's going on in this country, and particularly in Dublin, you do need to have a look at the goings-on down in the castle.

At the centre of all the juicy bits emanating from the tribunals over the last while is the one and only Frank Dunlop. His revelations to the Flood/Mahon tribunal have caused many a sleepless night for all manner of previously reasonably well-thought-of councillors, politicians, businessmen and property developers, and with good reason too. I remember well that fateful week a couple of years ago when Floody told him to go home and reflect on his position, and the following week Frank returned to the tribunal and sang like a canary. Much like a traditional *sean nós* purist, he's still singing, and could be for some time to come, but the verse I like the best is the one about the parcel of land out in north Dublin, in a place known as Drumnigh. This verse encapsulates, in a stand-alone incident, the kind of thing that has being going on for years, and will, in all probability, continue to go on well into the future. Why? Because very few people actually give a shit about such matters, and those that do give a shit rarely get a chance to do anything about it. I'll give you the abridged version.

In an article in *The Irish Times* on 22 October 2003, it was reported that Frank had met the now infamous G.V. Wright in the bar in Leinster House and handed him £2,000, which he had discreetly wrapped in a newspaper (quite possibly a copy of that morning's *Irish Times* and all, though the good folk in D'Olier Street would, I'm sure, omit that little detail from the article, lest it sully their good name any further). It was, according to Frank, a measure of his client's appreciation for Mr Wright's support for a rezoning motion, that client being one Mr Denis Mahony, a well-known businessman who had previously been involved with the Toyota franchise in Ireland and latterly in the Mount Juliet complex in Thomastown, Co. Kilkenny. Turns out that G.V. was one of four councillors on Dublin County Council who had been allegedly bribed – a charge he hotly denies – in return for their voting in favour of the rezoning of the lands at Drumnigh, out in Portmarnock. Obviously, Mr Wright and one of the other councillors mentioned, a Mr Seán Gilbride, strenuously deny any such allegations of impropriety, as did the other two councillors involved before their deaths several years ago, Messrs Cyril Gallagher and Jack Larkin.

After Denis Mahony had originally bought the 30-acre parcel of land in 1991 for £190,000, he hired Frank Dunlop to lobby the councillors on his behalf to get the lands rezoned. After all, what's the point in having a 30-acre parcel of land in north Dublin if you can't build a load of houses on it? And so Frank went to work. Now, 'lobbying' can be an altogether innocent activity, involving as it does the use of one's ability to persuade others to act in a way that would be of benefit to one's clients. Maybe he rang a few of the councillors and maybe he met a few others and politely suggested that rezoning the lands would be good for the local community in that it would create a few new jobs and all that crack, and left them to make up their own minds about the proposal's merits and await the outcome of the vote. But businessmen like Denis Mahony do not accumulate the wealth they have by leaving things to chance. They like to have the cards stacked in their favour. You know this, I know this, and Frank Dunlop certainly knew this and sensibly decided that given the world we live in and the way it works, it would be much easier to ensure the support of those councillors by slipping them a couple of grand in a wrapped-up newspaper.

And so in April 1993 the meeting went ahead, and guess what? The motion to rezone Mr Mahony's land was passed, with 28 votes for the motion and 11 against. The county manager recommended that the decision be reversed but at another meeting, in September 1993, the motion to reverse the decision was defeated by 28 votes to 24. Four votes. Isn't that gas? And this despite the fact that 2,530 objections had been lodged against the rezoning. But sure they were only from gobshites who lived in the area, people whose lives would be affected by the development, so obviously their opinion on the proposal didn't matter at all. Meanwhile, Denis Mahony kept his head down, said nothing and did nothing. Until 2000 that is, when he sold the rezoned lands to Seán Mulryans Ballymore Homes for a cool £13.5 million. For God's sake – bought in 1991 for £190,000, controversially rezoned in 1993 and sold in 2000 for £13.5 million. And the cute hoor had transferred ownership of the lands to his daughter before the sale so as to minimise the tax liability on the proceeds. I'd say she's a popular girl around town. With a lovely personality too, I'm sure. Then – this bit cracks me up – Frank met Denis in 1994, looking for a success fee for his help in getting the lands rezoned.

Denis allegedly asked him if all of the £10,000 had been used up in bribing, sorry lobbying, the councillors, and was aghast at how much the rezoning cost. Can you believe that? The guy had just netted over £13 million and was whining about throwing Frank a few grand as a thank you.

Mr Mahony was 'adamant' that he employed Frank on a professional basis as a lobbyist and knew nothing about payments to councillors. Why were they paid in cash then? Very few people in business settle invoices for £10,000 in cash. As Frank Dunlop said himself, Mr Mahony 'knew the way the world worked'. This implies that he was aware that money would have to be paid to the councillors to guarantee their support for the rezoning motion.

(One thing I don't get, though, is how the various councillors and Frank Dunlop were happy to take only a couple of grand here and there in return for their critical support for this and countless other motions. You see, I'm no angel and I can tell you, if I was a councillor and was approached to support a particular rezoning motion, I'd be looking for at least a hundred grand. If you're gonna risk hanging yourself out to dry, you may as well make it worth your while. Two grand? I don't think so.)

But *why* had Frank decided to grass up all the boys? Had to be something to do with money. When you're dealing with a certain type of person it pays to heed the advice of Jack Nicholson's Jake Gittes in Chinatown, and 'follow the money'. I'm glad to say that Barry O'Kelly, Crime Correspondent for *The Sunday Business Post*, saved me the hassle of doing the following by writing an article in the 2 November 2003 edition of the paper which threw considerable light on just why Frank Dunlop had turned states evidence and spilt the beans on what had been going on in the Dublin planning scene for the last number of years.

Turns out that Frank had become increasingly pissed off standing on the sidelines and watching the big boys make a fortune from his considerable lobbying skills in dealing with the pesky planners and had decided to have a go at the property lark himself. There was a 400-acre site out in Baldoyle that Frank, on behalf of a number of different landowners, previously, and unsuccessfully, had tried to get rezoned. Frank then took an option on the land himself, and decided to have another go at the rezoning. If he succeeded he would be stinking rich, but one G.V. Wright, who was the whip in the Fianna Fáil gang in Dublin City Council at the time, disapproved of Frank's plans and got in his way. (Yes, the very same G.V. Wright mentioned above in connection with the dodgy rezoning decision granted in favour of Denis O'Mahony's 30-acre parcel of land out in Portmarnock.) G.V. got his long-time ally Senator Don Lydon on board and the pair took it upon themselves to oppose Frank's rezoning application, and when the motion to rezone was sponsored, it was defeated, scuppering Frank's plans to at last catapult himself to mega riches. Justifiably really, I suppose, this prompted Frank to grass the pair up at the first available opportunity. Another lad who got in Frank's way is the one arm-bandit Jim Kennedy, one-time owner of an amusement arcade on Westmoreland Street, familiar I'm sure to many of you who bunked off school and dossed the day away in town. Jim, the cute bucko, had bought a key 10-acre site off the Grange Road, thus securing access to Frank's site and placing another obstacle in his way, because apparently without this 10-acre plot Frank would have faced serious problems in either developing or flogging the site for its maximum market value. Frank obviously made an offer to Jim but he wouldn't go for it and he sold the land on to Seán Mulryan, the main man behind Ballymore Homes, a serious property developer both here and in England.

So poor old Frank was screwed, nobody wanted to play with him, and he ended up selling his option on the land to Seán Mulryan as well for about €1 million. A million might sound like a lot of money, but the land has since been rezoned for 2,000 new homes and is estimated to be now worth in excess of €200 million. Sickener or what? So obviously Frank dobbed Big Jim in to the tribunal as well, claiming that Kennedy had given him £25,000 with which to bribe councillors for rezoning applications Kennedy had an interest in.

As I write this section I am licking my lips in anticipation of the forthcoming trial of Mr Ray Burke, former Minister for Justice, who is due to make an appearance in the Four Courts some time soon to answer charges brought against him by the Criminal Assets Bureau in relation to various anomalies that have come to light as a result of his 'co-operation' with the tribunals. Regardless of the outcome of the case, we quite possibly wouldn't have heard of such goings-on were it not for the actions of two largely unsung heroes, Mr Michael Smith and Mr Colm Mac Eochaidh, two Dublin-based barristers and conservationists. Disappointed that no government had the bottle to set up the tribunals we now finally have, the two boys decided to take matters into their own hands. They weren't looking for glory at all – they were actually seriously pissed off when *The Sunday Times* revealed their identities in January 1998 – they were just fed up with all the shit property development that was going on. The lads had previously set up a company called Lancefort and they used this vehicle to oppose and challenge planning decisions which they felt were going to be to the detriment of our architectural heritage, and in doing so gave the principals behind the likes of Zoe Developments and Treasury Holdings a complete pain in their respective arses. I liked them straight away, I have to say.

Then Michael and Colm decided to up the ante. They hatched a plan to offer a reward for information that might help them force the government's hand into finally establishing a proper forum for the investigation of matters of alleged corruption, rumours of which had been circulating for years and were now gathering substance. The two boys approached a couple of solicitors in Dublin to act on their behalf and be the conduit through which all the juicy information would flow, because obviously they didn't want to go public on it themselves. Nobody in town wanted to know about it, probably because it represented a conflict of interest, in that most of the solicitors in Dublin 2 were already up to their eyes looking after the affairs of their current clients, those same clients being the very people the boys were trying to get a hold of in the first place. So the lads cleverly headed north of the border and got in touch with a firm of solicitors by the name of Donnelly Neary and Donnelly in Newry, Co. Down. Everybody knows what northies are like, tight as a duck's arse, they'd do anything for a dollar, so this crowd said they'd act for them no problem, and promptly placed a little ad in the main Dublin newspapers, offering £10,000 for information on matters of corruption in Irish public life and what have you.

Given the shit that goes on in this place, you'd think they'd be inundated with mail the same way Gay Byrne used to be when there was a new car to be won in a postal quiz on The Late Late Show, back in the old days before people got notions about their vehicular and upward mobility and all bought new cars every two years. I'd say they got a good response alright, but the letter that mattered the most was from one Mr James Gogarty, the now legendary former executive of Joseph Murphy Structural Engineering, a company formerly based out in Santry in north Dublin. He felt he had been betrayed pension-wise by the Murphy clan when he retired after many years of discreet and active service and so happily dished the dirt on Ray Burke, and it was this information that was instrumental in the Flood tribunal being set up in the first place. So Mr Smith and Mr Mac Eochaidh, take a bow. Fair play to you both.

The Druimnigh tale recounted above serves to give you a flavour of the kind of thing that has made this country the great little nation it is today. It also gives us an insight into the activities of some of the members of Ireland's golden circle. I've long had an interest in these goings-on, principally because they give you a fair idea of how things work in a two-tier society such as ours, where on the lower tier sit the likes of you and me, for the most part ordinary decent citizens who work pretty hard to get ahead, and on the upper tier sit a couple of dozen businessmen who effectively run the country, dictating to compliant politicians what sort of policies and measures would be of most use to them in their efforts to make as much money as possible in as short a time as possible. This is, I am fully aware, not too dissimilar to the way many societies operate, as a glance at the scandals emerging on an almost daily basis in the US or Italy or the Middle East will attest to. But we don't live in the US or Italy or the Middle East so the ramifications of those dubious activities have little or no effect on us. However, the shit that goes on here does have a very real impact and effect on us, hitting us principally in our pockets, as we foot the €101-million-so-far-and-still-climbing tab for the legal bills incurred by the state in its investigation of allegedly corrupt matters.

And so, with your permission, I would like to take a very quick look at some of the privileged members of this 'golden circle', briefly outlining their connections with various political figures and the benefits accruing to them from such associations and relationships.

Some time later:

After consultation with my publishers, I have been informed that unfortunately it is not possible to reproduce on the next page a rather large gold circle with various names festooned around it, as per my original idea. This decision has been made in the light of two factors, the first being the increased production costs involved in repro-ducing golden-hued graphical illustrations, and the second being my failure to adhere to the delivery date for this manuscript, thereby limiting the time available to the production department and typesetters to include the aforementioned circular graphical illustration. Sorry about that, but may I suggest that you go through this chapter in much the same way as one would with a study aid, and take a sheet of blank paper and a pencil and follow the instructions as they appear? Kind of an interactive thing, I suppose, but I think you'll find it both a useful and wrath-inducing exercise. Pencils sharpened and at the ready? Away we go.

Take your pencil and draw a large circle with a radius of approximately four inches. If you are confident enough, you may do this freehand. Otherwise, use a compass to ensure a nice, neat circle. Ask an adult to help you, if necessary – we don't want any pricks! (The page will be full of them by the time we're finished anyway.) Now, starting at the topmost point of your circle, draw lots of smaller circles all around your big circle. It doesn't really matter how many you draw because you won't have enough room for all the names that could be used in an exercise such as this, due to the constantly evolving nature of the subject under discussion.

In each of these smaller circles you may insert some of the names of the multitude of businesspeople and politicians who have come to the attention of the media and the tribunals as a result of their sometimes dubious activities and the incestuous nature of some of their relationships, which in relation to matters of the state, should remain impartial and at arms length. Depending on where in the country you live, or what your political allegiances are, or what newspapers, if any, you read, the names you might suggest for inclusion in this little exercise may differ slightly from the ones I have in mind. This matters not a jot: the main purpose of the exercise is simply to remind ourselves that we have arrived at a point in Irish life where this kind of carry on is what passes for normal business practice. Though in possession of some juicy bits of info which I would very much like to reveal to you, I'd never get them past the legal bods who will be scanning through this manuscript in a couple of weeks time, so I will restrict myself to reporting very briefly on matters that are already in the public domain. Due to pressure on space, some further research of your own may be necessary to fully appreciate all the ins and outs of the shenanigans this shower of crooks get up to, but it would be time well spent, I think, especially in the run-up to local and general elections. I'll happily kick start the thing for you, though.

So, in the first circle, let us put the name Bertie Ahern. Apart from overseeing the recent mismanagement of the economy, the decimation of the public services and the series of U-turns in relation to pre-election promises, there is no evidence of any wrongdoing or impropriety on the part of Bertie. What there *is* plenty of, though, is evidence that he must have had a fair idea of what was going on when Charlie Haughey was up to his old tricks. A serious blot on his copybook was when Charlie Haughey's former private secretary, Ms Eileen Foy, revealed to the Moriarty tribunal that Bertie, in his capacity as co-signatory of cheques drawn on the party leader's allowance, which is provided by the Exchequer (i.e. you), had *pre-signed* most of the cheques for Charlie to do with as he wished. A suspiciously large number of these cheques were made out in very round numbers, something that would be unusual for an account which was supposed to be used for operational expenses. When did you last get a telephone bill for exactly €100? Or a bill from a printing supplier for exactly €1,500? And why would a lot of these cheques have been made out for cash when they were supposed to be used to pay bills on foot of an invoice being presented? For instance, one cheque drawn on account number 30208/062, made payable to cash, co-signed by Bertie Ahern and dated 16 June 1989 was for the sum of £25,000. For instance, one cheque drawn on account number 30208/062, made payable to cash, co-signed by Bertie Ahern and dated 4 April 1991 was for the sum of £5,000. For instance, one cheque drawn on account number 30208/062, co-signed by Bertie Ahern and dated 11 September 1991 was for the sum of £10,000. And so on. I must stress that not all of the cheques drawn on this account were used for cash withdrawals. No, a good number of them were used to pay for lavish meals in Le Coq Hardi restaurant or for tailored shirts from Charvet in Paris. And when the Labour party tried to have the use of the Fianna Fáil party leader's allowance included in the terms of reference of the Moriarty tribunal, and tabled a motion calling for such an inclusion, it was defeated. *Quelle surprise*, as they say in France. Bertie Ahern is of course also the man who displayed a remarkable talent for character assessment by appointing none other than Mr Liam Lawlor to the Dáil's ethics committee. Stop laughing. This is serious.

That's enough about Bertie. In the next circle, I'd suggest we put the name of one Des Richardson. Des is a man with apparently remarkable powers of persuasion and he put these talents to good use in his former role as chief fundraiser for Fianna Fáil from 1993 until 1999. Out of the kindness of his heart, he still gives generously of his time to the party every year at that most crucial time, the weeks preceding and during the Galway Races, which nets about €150,000 every year for GCHQ in Drumcondra, I mean Lower Mount Street. A great man for the old consulting too, was Des. A bit like The Godfather, I suppose. You had a problem, you went to see Des, told him all about it, and in return for a modest fee, he'd advise you on the best course of action. Take Risk Management International (RMI), for example. For some time, Des received a grand a month from this security firm for much needed consultancy advice on how to source and secure new clients. Happily, Des's advice was bang on the money, and I'm pleased to report that RMI's client base grew. It has also been in receipt of a number of government contracts at various times, but a director of the company has made it pointedly clear that Des was of no assistance whatsoever in securing this particular business. The company that seemed to consume a lot of Des's time as a director, though, was one called Berraway Ltd. Funnily enough, whilst on the surface Berraway didn't seem to do a whole lot, it had shed loads of cash going through its bank account: nearly a million pounds in fact, from August 1996 to early 2000. Lovely jubbly.

In my next circle I'll put in the name of John Finnegan, of Finnegan Menton on Merrion Row in Dublin 2. Johnny first came to unwanted public attention back in the early 1990s with the whole Telecom scandal down in Ballsbridge. He had advised the state company on where in Ballsbridge the building was exactly, and subsequently requested a 'finder's fee' of £150,000 for his trouble. He graciously settled for £40,000 when his old pal Mick Smurfit – then both the chairman of Telecom Éireann *and* a beneficiary of all the shit that went on with the eventual acquisition of the Johnston Mooney O'Brien site by Telecom for £9.4 million – intervened and told him to cop on a bit. Then, in 1999, it emerged that John had been the beneficiary of a loan to the tune of £1.88 million, this loan being secured by way of substantial Ansbacher deposits. And then the Flood tribunal asked him in for a cup of tea to explain his involvement with a Guernesy-based company called Foxtown Investments. Foxtown and two other companies controlled by those two huckster property developers Tom Brennan and Joseph McGowan (who built Ray Burke's house in Swords for free), all owned equal shares in a company called Ardcarn Ltd, which in turn wholly owned yet another Channel Islands company called Canio Ltd, right? Canio had been set up to buy some land up in Sandyford, Co. Dublin, and between 1984 and 1985 it made two payments totalling £75,000 to a company owned by Ray Burke. (Guess what Ray's company was called? Caviar Ltd.) Once again, I must stress that I'm not suggesting that John Finnegan knew that a company he was associated with was involved in making these highly irregular payments to Ray Burke. Sure you can't go wrong with bricks and mortar.

Speaking of bricks and mortar, may I propose property magnate John Byrne as the occupier of our next circle? Allegedly 'invited' by Seán Lemass to return from England to construct big, ugly office blocks to house expanding government departments, John Byrne took up the commission with considerable gusto. The resulting property portfolio now nets him something like €1.9

million in rent every year. The various tenants of his buildings include, believe it or not, the Revenue Commissioners, who are involved in ongoing investigations of Ansbacher account holders. A quick phone call to their landlord might be in order, for it is none other than Johnny Byrne who was identified as one of the largest Ansbacher account holders. Irish Intercontinental Bank has issued something like €30 million in loans to two of his main operating vehicles, Carlise Trust Ltd and Alstead Securities, security for these loans taking the form of the healthy deposits Johnny had lodged with Ansbacher in the Cayman Islands. This is the 'back-to-back' method of raising finance, where the bank giving you the loan would accept the undeclared cash you had stashed offshore as security for the loan, whilst helpfully omitting from the facility letter for the loan the fact that such an arrangement was in place, lest the meddlesome civil servants in the Revenue got a whiff of what was going on.

In 1988 Johnny made a killing when a hotel he has a controlling interest in, The Mount Brandon in Tralee, was inexplicably included in the *urban* renewal scheme. Now, without wishing to upset the good people of Tralee in any way, I think it's safe to say that it hardly constitutes an urban area in the same way that Dublin or Galway would. Then when Haughey was Taoiseach Johnny got another boost in 1990 when his Tara Street baths site on Townsend Street – which he had been sitting on for about 20 years – was also designated for urban renewal, replete with the standard tax-incentives of course.

The Don was eventually called to appear before the Moriarty tribunal to answer questions in relation to his alleged extraordinary generosity towards Charlie Haughey throughout his 'career'. At the tribunal, Johnny said, 'I'd like to categorically state that I have never given Mr Haughey a penny or a pound in my life.' Funny that, really, because a loan that one of Johnny's companies, Prince's Trust, paid off in 1987 by way of lodging £186,986 sterling into an account in Guinness & Mahon, actually ended up in an account controlled by the one and only Des Traynor, who was Johnny's auditor and investment adviser, and of course Charlie Haughey's lap dog, arranging all sorts of handouts for him over the years from Ireland's business elite. Probably just a clerical error, though.

So that's Johnny Byrne. Next up is that old self-styled codger, Jim Mansfield, owner of the Citywest complex. Jim's a bit of a chancer, but most of his exploits have paid off rather handsomely. He started off in the car trade, working out of a place called Crooksling in Saggart. Things went a bit pear-shaped early on for Big Jim though, and he did a three-month stretch in prison in 1958 for petty theft, and then in the early 1960s he did two more stretches in the nick – one for receiving a stolen car, and one for ten counts of larceny. Survivor that he is, though, he put all that behind him with the success of his company Truck & Machinery Sales, which made a fortune salvaging all the earth-moving equipment left over from the Falklands war in the early 1980s. The proceeds from this sweet deal helped him buy the 164-acre farm in Saggart for about a million, and with all that he's since developed on it, it's reckoned to be now worth about €350 million. His working capital requirements got a timely boost in 1985 when he got himself over £4 million in loans from Des Traynor's

Ansbacher operation, and then in 2000 he bought a further 800 acres of land just down the road in Johnstown for about €13 million; which with the right zoning is probably now worth about €150 million. He got into a bit of trouble there a while back for throwing up a convention centre without first obtaining planning permission. But Jim only had the best interest of the country at heart – he wanted to get the place fitted out in time to land a few juicy conferences during Ireland's EU presidency earlier this year. He was sure to get them as well, having previously hosted the Fianna Fáil Ard Fheis in his hotel. Sure, it was the least they could do after the hefty donations he made to the party.

Then we have Mick Bailey of Bovale Developments, generous supporter of Fianna Fáil, and the man who was so good as to help them out as it made enquiries into the Ray Burke affair after the last election. After dragging his feet for some time, Mick eventually conceded to the Flood tribunal that he had indeed given the not inconsiderable sum of £30,000 to Mr James Gogarty, who had then passed the money on to Ray Burke. Despite his willingness to co-operate fully with all relevant phases of the tribunal, in a most unfortunate turn of events, many of Mick's meticulous financial records were destroyed in a fire on the *very day* that the Supreme Court was to decide on the validity of an order made by the tribunal requesting Mick to hand them over. Pity that. And in The Second Interim Report of the Tribunal of Inquiry into Certain Planning Matters and Payments (bit of a mouthful that, isn't it?), which was published in September 2002 (and available to buy for only €1, which is great value, running as it does to

402 pages. Rip-off Ireland my arse!), it was stated that the tribunal was satisfied that Michael Bailey's wife, Ms Caroline Bailey, 'hindered and obstructed' the tribunal by failing to comply with Orders for Discovery, by failing to 'provide a truthful account as to the existence of bank accounts held in her name at Bank of Ireland, Phibsboro and Bank of Ireland, Swords', and by 'preparing a notebook, said to record payments to Mr James Gogarty, which she knew to be a false document'. There's a pair of them in it, alright.

Do you notice a pattern developing here? Good. I'll do one more and then leave you to work on the rest of the project yourselves. Who will I go for now? Let me see … no, I can't do him, it'd take about ten pages, can't do him 'cos he's a cantankerous bastard and will probably sue me … so it'll have to be … him, yeah, he'll do. Step forward Owen O'Callaghan. Cork-based O'Callaghan's name is cropping up down in Dublin Castle at the moment in relation to his involvement in the Quarryvale development out on the Lucan road, where the Liffey Valley complex now sits. O'Callaghan is alleged to have doled out over £1m to Frank Dunlop so that he could grease the necessary wheels when getting the planning sorted out for the huge site, which he took over from Tom Gilmartin, the man who claims to have given £50,000 to that gobshite Pee Flynn. A funny thing happened on the morning of the government's last day in office back in 1994 when the Fianna Fáil/Labour coalition collapsed. It designated a site – in Athlone of all places – for urban renewal. On its *last* day in office. Who owned the site? None other than Mr O'Callaghan, in partnership with another lad from

Limerick who owned a company called Tiernan Properties. I'm sure it was just a coincidence and all that, just one of those things they had meant to get around to before then but never found the time. O'Callaghan has been a significant donor to the Fianna Fáil party machine over the years and such generosity has been handsomely rewarded. What goes around, comes around, as they say.

In your remaining blank circles you could, for obvious reasons, insert the names of Liam Lawlor, Jim Kennedy, Ray Burke, Ben Dunne, Michael Lowry, Tom Brennan, Joseph McGowan, Oliver Barry … you get the idea. I'll only get annoyed if I fill you in on every last dodgy deal that these lads have been involved in, so I'll leave it at that.

To complete the exercise, simply colour in the gaps between the names with a gold coloured highlighter. For added effect, you could dab some play glue around the circle and sprinkle some gold glitter on it.

So that's the golden circle, in seriously abridged form. Next I want to have a quick look at the 'ramifications' faced by a few political figures whose suspicious antics and close links to a number of businessmen have brought them to the attention of the voting public. Ramifications may be the wrong word to use, though, in that it implies that some sort of sanction would be forthcoming to the bold boys in question, that they would be made to go and stand in the corner or something, or be declared ineligible to accompany their friends on the next outing, or something like that. Not a bit of it.

John Ellis, a Fianna Fáil TD in the Sligo-Leitrim area, was the recipient of £12,000 from Charlie Haughey in

1989, and a further £13,600 in 1990. These monies came from the party leader's account, which is public money, that is *your* money. The funds were apparently withdrawn from AIB using cheques that had apparently been pre-signed by Bertie Ahern, which was handy. Johnny was also the principal behind a meat company that collapsed a while back in the 1980s. In November 1999, as a little slap on the wrist, he bowed to pressure to resign as chairman of the Joint Oireachtas Committee on Agriculture, Food and the Marine, which was a lot easier than having to nurse a loss of £300,000, which was the fate of the 80 or so farmers his company owed money to. After some of these farmers made calls for the bills to be paid, John Boy, decent skin that he is, eventually managed to cough up about £120,000 to the Irish Farmers Association, and this money was disbursed to the seriously pissed off farmers. John has since got into the property game, and recently secured planning permission for fifteen houses on his farm near Carrick-on-Shannon, the proceeds from which should keep him going for a while. Terrifyingly, John Ellis took 92.6 per cent of the Fianna Fáil vote in Leitrim, leading the poll with 7,051 votes.

Denis Foley, another Fianna Fáil TD, was revealed to have been the holder of an Ansbacher account for a long period of time, and decided not to stand for re-election the last time round. After Ellis's performance I'd say he was raging. And out west in Mayo, despite being found to have colluded in tax evasion by her peers, Ms Beverley Cooper-Flynn was re-elected as an official Fianna Fáil candidate.

Michael Lowry, after all his carry on with Ben Dunne and house extensions here and there and what not, was easily re-elected on the first count last time round, capturing more than 25 per cent of the total vote in his constituency in Tipperary North.

With all this, you'd think that even Liam Lawlor regretted not chancing his arm and standing for re-election. Whoever coined the phrase 'all politics is local' really knew his stuff, for that would appear to be the way of it here alright. Screw up all you like, pull as many strokes as you can, but get us an aul hospital or an odd factory in the town and we'll see you right come election time. Sure, that was then, and this is now, no point in looking back, is there?

I'm sure there are many politicians who sincerely hope the electorate sticks to that opinion.

The Happiness Thing

Happiness, for at least one person I know, is apparently, a Hamlet cigar. Or rather, being left alone for a couple of hours to prepare a meal whilst listening to a CD player, the radio, reading three newspapers and watching the TV all at the same time whilst enjoying a Hamlet cigar is his idea of happiness. And who I am to argue with that? Whatever floats your boat. Me, I have a pretty good idea of what makes me happy too. The only problem is that my idea of happiness is so absolute and inflexible that unless all the ingredients pertaining to my idea of happiness conjoin in an environmentally compatible manner at the exact point in time when I am most amenable to receiving them, it just doesn't work. Needless to say, such an intoxicating state of perfect harmony has presented itself to me on only a very small number of occasions. Three, in fact, that I can remember with absolute certainty. Some people might feel that this is a terrifying realisation to face up to as one approaches mid-life. I don't, however, partly because to do so would indeed be quite terrifying, but mostly because, after having spent longer than is probably advisable considering the matter, I am satisfied with the formula I have devised, and am therefore content to let it arise, however intermittently.

These three occasions when I knew I was definitely happy all shared a number of characteristics. One of these was an acceptance that fate had played a huge part in bringing about this wondrous confluence of ingredients, that they were uniquely applicable to me, and that if I did not act on them there and then, they would quickly disappear, never to return again. The most important though was the absence of an ingredient closely associated with happiness – money. I know everybody needs a certain amount of cash every month to keep the wolf from the door, but an unexpected cash influx was not a factor in my attaining that state of happiness on any of those occasions. In fact, quite the reverse held, in that given my self-employed status for the last ten years or so and the lack of holiday pay and/or sick pay such status entails, my acting on fate's intervention in my life actually resulted in a monetary loss.

To give you an example. In October 2001, I was, I hate to admit, in Renards nightclub. They were, however, extenuating circumstances. At the time I was wrapping up my foolhardy involvement in a feature film which had consumed my time and resources for the previous fifteen months or so. Things were looking very bad for the prospects of the film and I was seriously pissed off. Then, within the space of two days, I managed to get an agent in London to handle international sales for the film and was also told that it had been selected for exhibition in that month's Cork International Film Festival. A night out was called for, if only for the release it would provide after so many dark months of uncertainty, and so a group of us went off on the beer and had the crack. We ended up in Renards about one in the morning and went downstairs, where we quickly got separated. Keen to conduct myself properly in such a rarefied environment, I availed of the solidly constructed bar counter as a support and proceeded to sip away at a few libations, watching my colleagues and others gyrate pathetically on the dance floor. A young woman approached the bar and attempted to squeeze in beside me to order a drink. Not enjoying much success, after a minute or so she asked me if I would shout for a drink for her.

'Glass of water for the lady, please,' I said to the barman, in what probably appeared to be a most arrogant manner, as though he were present only to attend to my every whim, but was in fact, the only way I could fulfil her request with the minimum of discourse, my capacity for it having been severely debilitated as a result of the sustained drinking session I had been on for the previous six or seven hours, something I was not very accustomed to, or, as I was slowly realising, able for.

At this point, I hadn't even deigned to look at the water-requesting woman, figuring that as I had enjoyed a pretty good night thus far, I didn't want to spoil it by finding her to be to my liking, in that, more likely than not, she was present in the club with some boorish jock south county Dublin asshole she hadn't yet recognised as such. The glass of water duly arrived, but I noticed that its recipient didn't disappear.

'You look like you don't want to be here anymore than I do,' she then said.

To me. As I turned to face her, my alcoholically depleted cognitive capacities rebooted and informed me that she was in fact, to use the common parlance, chatting me up. What other reason could there be? She asked me to get her a glass of water; I got her a glass of water. Our business was concluded, and yet she remained. I was, however, sure there would be something about her that I fundamentally didn't like which would register with me in no less than seven seconds, and so as I turned to reply to her, it was my sole intention to refrain from being an asshole, exchange pleasantries for a moment, then politely make my excuses and repair to the bathroom to see if I could throw up before I slipped off without saying goodbye to those I had arrived with and attempted to get a taxi home.

Eight seconds later, I was devastated to acknowledge to myself that far from finding anything remotely unattractive about her I was utterly smitten with her. Both of us quickly explained to each other the mitigating circumstances that led us to be in the club in the first place (mine being eminently more plausible than hers, I have to say, but this was something I was content to overlook). Such explanations conveniently allowed us to proceed on to trade barbed comments about the club and its occupants for a few minutes, castigating all around us who were foolish enough to think they were having a good time and that even if there was an alternative universe outside that contained within it the comfortable environs of Grafton Street and its immediate surrounds, it couldn't be any better than this. We then moved on to the whole 'what do you do?' thing, which is a question I have always found difficult to answer without sounding either vague or naïvely aspirational. I told her about the film thing and it turned out she knew some producers around town and blah, blah, blah. She was very coy about her own occupation, though, which intrigued me, but I didn't press her on it.

And then next thing I know, she's gone. One of her friends came up and whisked her away, saying they were off home, and that was that. No number, just a name, and however unlikely it was that I would forget such a name, it wasn't much to go on if I were to stand any chance of seeing her again. I shrugged it off and went to the bathroom – where I was very successful in throwing up – and slipped off without saying goodbye to anyone.

So I went to Cork the following week for the film festival, met loads of complete morons and got pissed for free for a couple of nights. Came back to Dublin and the following weekend was having a read of *The Sunday Business Post* when I see a photograph of the same woman I had met in Renards the previous week. She was receiving some design award for her recently opened business in town. This just got better. Not only was she cynical, disparaging and seriously cute, but she was also making her own way in the world running her own business, and quite successfully too, apparently. The next day, I rang her place of work to get her mobile number and texted her a funny little message. She replied in kind and after some toing and froing on this level, we progressed to a real verbal conversation, the result of which was me convincing her that we should go out to dinner the following week. We did, and it was great. I met her in The Globe on South Great Georges Street, where she was smart enough to be more than fashionably late and ring me as she came in so she would recognise me again. We had a drink and then slipped around the corner to Odessa for dinner. Conversation flowed like we were old friends catching up after not seeing each other for years, and we covered a lot of ground, most crucially agreeing that both kids and the institution of marriage were highly overrated and to be avoided at all costs.

What a cool chick, this could really go somewhere, I was thinking to myself. Until that was, our conversation continued in her car on the way home – where she scored even more brownie points by being an excellent driver, assuredly doing sixty along the dual carriageway out to Bray – when she informed me that as well as having no interest in marriage or children, she also had no interest in going out with me on any kind of serious basis. Not just me, in fact, which would have been totally understandable, but anybody at all. She had decided to focus solely on making a success of her fledgling business interests, and was more than happy to sacrifice the highs and lows a personal relationship entailed in her pursuit of that goal. Admirable as her determination was, this position didn't suit me in the slightest: I had already stepped over the line and allowed myself be smitten by her. I knew she liked me too, because she had told me just before declaring herself unavailable, so I wasn't keen at all on not having things move on any further than this.

We arrived in Bray and I bade her goodnight, resisting the urge to jump on her in the hope of having the opportunity to do so at a later stage in a more conducive environment than that presented by the confines of her car. We went out together a couple of nights more, each one more enjoyable than the last, each one ending with her declaring that she didn't want to get involved with anyone, and me ignoring such declarations in the hope of eventually wearing her down. The dreaded Christmas period rolled around and she told me that she would be spending it with her family in Cork, of all bloody places. I took it on the chin, reckoning that that was indeed that, and that the new year would render me the sole inhabitant of Dumpsville.

And so imagine my surprise and elation when I get a call from her on New Year's Eve, telling me that she was on her way back from Cork and wanted to know if I fancied calling over to her otherwise unoccupied place to watch a movie. I was still driving a taxi at the time, trying to pay off a few bills from the whole movie fiasco, and was just heading down through Bray to begin what was bound to be an undoubtedly lucrative night, however taxing on my mental reserves it would no doubt prove to be, involving as it would dealing with an inordinate amount of assholes in search of the greatest night of their pathetic lives. I casually acquiesced to her suggestion and promptly executed a three-point turn on the main street of Bray village and tore back up the Vevay Road to the house where I quickly showered and changed before selecting a few choice movies from my landlord's video collection.

On arrival at her stylish home, I was greeted with a level of affection and warmth that could definitely have been classified as inappropriate coming from someone so resolutely of the opinion that she didn't want to go out with anyone. I felt it would be churlish and impolite to make this point, so I didn't. We settled down on the sofa with a bottle of wine and watched the videos I had brought with me. (Even more brownie points scored here, after she declared

Magnolia one of the best films she had ever seen.) Anyway, suffice to say that a fantastic night was had by all, and I left her house very early the following morning about four hundred pounds poorer. Such a realisation was more than compensated for by the marked increase in the spring in my step, however.

And so on that particular night, 31 December 2001, I attained a state of happiness, and money played no part in it; indeed the foregoing of what was a substantial amount of money to me at the time was an essential concession I had to make to enjoy the night so much. Moreover, a couple of years prior to 2001, I know that I would not have made the choice I made on that night, because money was all important to me, and a huge determinant in me assessing the level of my own personal happiness index. At that time I had a cool apartment, a nice Merc and a few quid in the bank. I thought that this was what happiness was all about, and was therefore understandably both quite perplexed and seriously pissed off when I finally realised that far from being happy, I was actually quite *un*happy. So I sold the apartment and the Merc, took a year and a half off and spent all the money co-writing and producing a feature film, something I always wanted to do. The film didn't turn out to be the critically or commercially acclaimed masterpiece I had naïvely hoped it would be, but the process of actually doing something that I had always wanted to do made me happy.

Truth be told, I have been putting off starting this chapter for ages; principally because seeing as how it's the last one, it's supposed to encapsulate everything I've been talking about for the last hundred and fifty pages in one strong, well-reasoned argument. That's not necessarily going to happen – I'll try, but I'm knackered and really I want to just finish up and piss off to France to go camping for the summer. In the other chapters I've discussed various discrete and distinct topics and posed a few questions as to why things are the way they are, drawing on my own not insignificant number of encounters with the good, the bad and the ugly of Irish society as I tried to support my opinions with anecdotal evidence. Here, however, I am supposed to bring all that cumulative thought and talk to a heady conclusion and, God help me, maybe even come up with some answers! That's why I've avoided starting this final chapter until a few weeks before I have to have the bloody book finished.

Another reason, and equally important to my mind, was that I simply didn't know what title to put on the chapter itself. That might sound like a lame excuse to you, but I just find it easier to talk about something once I have decided on a title for that particular section. I suppose I hope it will help me put some kind of structure on the ramblings that follow me typing the chapter title. Doesn't always work out that way, but there you go – that's the logic behind it. And at first glance, whilst The Happiness Thing may not appear to be indicative of a very committed or productive thought process, I assure you it is. That's partly because it's in keeping with all the other 'Thing' chapter titles I have come up with thus far, but mainly because when you think about it – as I have while I've struggled through these pages – happiness, our own interpretation and pursuit of same, is really what life's all about. To be happy. What else is there?

It's not the same as 'pleased' or 'contented' or 'satisfied' or 'comfortable'. Somehow those words sound either noncommittal or vague, but 'happiness' is unequivocal and all-encompassing, and really, even with a language as expansive and versatile as English, there is no adequate substitute for it.

Then when I was flicking through a few old issues of *The Dubliner* magazine, I reread an article written by Ed Brophy in his Political Fictions column. Ed had come across some papers, research and articles detailing the work of one Mr Daniel Kahnmann, a Nobel prize winner for his work on the relationship between psychology and economics, and one Professor Richard Layard, he of the London School of Economics and another very well regarded figure in the study of such matters as personal well-being and economic development.

Sounded good, so I clicked on to Google and searched for some more info on the boys. I got loads of hits for Professor Layard and only a few for Mr Kahnmann, so I chose to focus on the work of Prof. Layard. I downloaded a few of his essays and speeches and read them whilst enjoying a smoke. Thoroughly as well, I might add – the more I read about his work the more interesting I found it. He's one smart cookie, this lad. Everything he says makes perfect sense to me. And to Tony Blair as well, evidently, for Prof. Layard was one of the principal architects of Labour's much-vaunted 'New Deal' initiative a few years back. No doubt, as is the way with all things governmental, some of his recommendations were either omitted, pared back or fine tuned in the interests of making the lives of those who had to implement the initiative less onerous, but the essence of the welfare-to-work deal makes sense. Anyway, according to Professor Layard, the things that affect people's happiness the most are, 'mental health, satisfying and secure work, a secure and loving private life, a safe community, freedom and moral values'. Now, apart from being fairly obvious when you study it, the compilation of this list has no doubt been the culmination of many years' hard work on the part of Mr Layard, so I'm quite content to use it as my starting point. This might appear to be something of a reversal of the original premise of the book, in that whilst I was supposed to look at why people seem to be *un*happy at the moment, the more I thought about it, it appeared more beneficial to try and evaluate what makes people happy in the first place and see what's missing. And anyway, if I just asked myself the question, 'Why are so many people unhappy at the moment?', all I'd have to do is say something like …

People are unhappy with the bin tax, and the grief the Luas and the Port Tunnel and the proposed metro cause them as they drive to work, and the bullshit spin that politicians put on their every failing and U-turn, and the sight of homeless people sleeping rough in a city so wealthy as Dublin, and the thoughts of getting a taxi home when they're pissed, and how the price of a cup of coffee has tripled in as many years because it is now called a latte grande and comes with a corrugated cardboard sleeve around it, and the way the health service is in such a shambles with people lying on trolleys for days on end waiting to be attended to by an overworked doctor who could make an incorrect decision as a result of the effects of sleep deprivation, and the state of some of the primary schools around the country where kids have to ask permission of the family of rodents occupying what passes for a bathroom before going about their business, and the fact that our neighbours in the UK can get insured on a car for what we pay in road tax alone, and the way that when we do pay our road tax and insurance and start driving we quickly realise that the roads are in shit anyway, and the fact that not one of the legion of politicians that has been shown up to being a lying, cheating bastard has gone to jail, and that you can't even have a smoke in a pub now after denying your first-born a college education to afford the price of the pint in the first place, and that if the media constantly tells us that things are so great why is it that we don't feel so great, and the fact that teenage scumbags can give the two fingers to the judicial system whilst ordinary decent people get their licence endorsed for doing 33 in a 30, and that present-day wannabes who are nothing but tomorrow's has-beens are lionised as the epitome of self-actualisation, and that the public services which are supposed to be the backbone of the country's infrastructure are run by quangos staffed by close associates of politicians who know jack shit about the area they are given responsibility for, and the fact that all politics is local and a TD can screw up on the national stage and get comfortably re-elected as long as he's managed to funnel a few quid into the locality, and the commandeering of events such as the Special Olympics by the government for its own promotion with bullshit rhetoric about how much they are doing for the less able in our society and how much they promise to do in the future, and the sudden reneging on such promises when the cameras have been switched off, and that our need to remain competitive in the face of growing economic uncertainty in the international marketplace means that people already working hard in unfulfilling jobs which they could lose on the basis of a spreadsheet generated thousands of miles away are now expected to work even harder and see less of their families and loved ones, and that hypocritical, amoral politicians schedule attendance at mass as a form of canvassing, and that all manner of neglect and abuse of those most vulnerable in our society receives a fraction of the attention it should, and …

And I'd be done, and I could book my ferry crossing to Roscoff. But that wouldn't really be the right way to do it, because that list of things about which people are unhappy, which is by no means exhaustive, is nothing new in itself. There has to be more to it than that. Every country has to deal with that kind of shit to a greater or lesser degree than we do. So if, as I suggested before, I start from the other end of the equation and work backwards, maybe, just maybe I'll come across what the x factor contributing to this air of disenchantment, this *un*happiness, is. Not promising anything now, this ain't Oprah, just me thinking out loud.

Before I get started, I better do the money thing first, in that I'm sure some of you may be scratching your heads at the fact that it doesn't feature on the professor's list. As I suggested in the little story that opened this chapter, which is reprinted with kind permission from the author – me – from my never-to-be-released *Diary of a Serial Under-Achiever in Matters of the Heart, Vol. II,* money isn't the be-all and end-all when it comes to being happy. I'm sure I'm not alone in this view, and believe me, I used to hold the complete opposite view – as I also mentioned above – and I used to hate hearing people saying, 'Oh, money isn't everything you know', principally because they invariably had shit loads of it.

Now, obviously, you don't need to be a Nobel Prize winner to deduce that on average, rich people are happier than poor people, but really they can be so in the long term only on an *individual* basis, which you may think is fine and dandy if you are that individual, but unless you live in total isolation on your own island, you can't escape the effects of living in a poor society, no matter how rich you are, and over time exposure to those effects is gonna wear you down and you won't actually be happy, so there.

You see, it's been shown that highly developed western societies – that means us folks, believe it or not – have *not* grown measurably happier than less well-off, developing countries as a result of the vastly different growth rates in our income. On the contrary, apparently, symptoms of unhappiness – suicides and demands for treatments for depression and the like – are on the increase in these allegedly more advanced societies. And the fruits of many years' research on the subject by Professor Layard and others have established that there is a distinct positive correlation between income and happiness, but *only* up to an income level of $15,000. (We're talking globally here, people, big picture stuff. I know the $15,000 mark sounds woefully inadequate in an Irish context, so up it to whatever you want to allow for the fact that we're all getting ripped off here, but just go with me on this for a bit, it makes a lot of sense.) So, if you're earning $10,000 one year and you get to $11,000 the next year, you're going to be markedly happier than you were before. And so on until your earnings hit the $15,000 mark. But once you get past the $15,000 earnings level, further increases in your income aren't necessarily gonna make you any happier, okay?

Why is this? Because people constantly revise upwards the norm they use to compare their incomes against. And two different but inter-related things drive up this norm. The first of these is their actual income, which itself accustoms them to higher standards of living. Habituation, Mr Layard calls it. It's a basic human phenomenon, and works for all things, good and bad. The second thing that drives up the norm is the level of income enjoyed by one's peers, the old Jones next door thing. Whilst most people would like to be on the kind of easy money enjoyed by the likes of TDs and MEPs, they are more likely to actually measure their own income against that of a 'reference group' they are familiar with – college mates, family members, friends working on the same industrial estate, that kind of thing, because these are people whose wage expectations they can identify with. And so if they find that their own income, relative to the number of hours they work, the responsibility their job entails and the level of grief they get from their boss stacks up okay with the incomes enjoyed by these members of their reference group, people are likely to be pretty happy with their situation.

However, if people change the boundaries of their reference group, it can be disastrous for their happiness levels. For example, in what was east Germany, income levels have risen dramatically since 1990, but happiness levels have dropped big time. Why? Because now that they're part of the capitalist European system, the east

Germans compare their incomes with those of their fellow west Germans, not the poor bastards still stuck in the old Soviet bloc countries they were previously ideologically aligned to. You can expect the same thing to happen in some of the accession states that are now part of our enlarged European Union too. The same thing has happened with working women in the US. Not hookers, you moron – women who work outside the home, as opposed to solely inside the home. As the historic gaps between the earnings of men and women have narrowed, you'd think that the women would now be happier. But the evidence suggests that they are not, because whereas before, they'd compared their incomes with other women, now that the boundaries of their reference group have been expanded to include men, they focus on the gap between the incomes of the different sexes that remain, and they're pissed off.

So far, so good, I hope? So we get used to these increases in our income on a yearly basis and consequently, every year we revise upwards the income level that we need to earn the following year to convince ourselves that we are happy. So let's say that in 2002 you earned exactly €28,000 and you were happy with that, okay? And looking forward to 2003 you reckoned that, to allow for inflation and a general feeling that you were moving onwards and upwards, you needed to earn say, €30,000, okay? And then the end of 2003 rolls around and you do the sums and realise that you did indeed earn exactly €30,000, but you're not happy at all because, to your horror, you discover that most of your peers earned say, €38,000 in that same year, for doing pretty much the same type and amount of work. You're pissed off and consequently revise your estimate for happiness-related earnings for the year 2004 sharply upwards, by a greater percentage than that which you would have used had you allowed yourself to be happy with your own successfully achieved income level and used a more proportionate percentage increase for the year ahead.

Now you may well achieve this new, much higher income level in 2004, but will you be happier than you were at the end of 2003? Not likely, if like most of the working population in Ireland, your ability to achieve a higher level of income is dependent on either doing lots of overtime, getting a promotion that involves more responsibility, or putting up with a longer commute to change jobs altogether. There are only twenty-four hours in a day, so if the number of hours you spend working increases as a result of your self-imposed demands for a higher income, then something's gotta give. Maybe you won't be able to help out with training your son's under-twelve football team on a Thursday evening like you had promised because that's when the overtime shift is available. Maybe you won't be able to meet the girls for your regular Tuesday night dinner and gossip sessions anymore because that's the night of the new evening classes at the institute you have to attend to get the promotion you need which will give you the income increase you have set yourself.

See what I mean? You can't have it every way, and there is plenty of evidence to suggest that even achieving these new, higher income levels isn't going to make us happy because as soon as we get it, we see someone with more than us and we re-define our base level again, and consequently need more the following year. And more, and more. And the more we chase it the more personal sacrifices are involved until it gets to the stage that we are literally getting up, going to work, coming home, five or six days a week, and then getting blind drunk on Friday and Saturday to forget all about it and watching a movie on Sunday to wind down and help us face up to doing it all over again.

So even though Americans are much richer than the Danes, for example, they are also less happy. If you've visited both countries, as I've been lucky enough to, I'm sure you can vouch for this. In America, it's all about money. Nothing else matters. A meritocracy they call it, where, allegedly, regardless of origin or circumstance, everyone has the inalienable right to work hard and rise to whatever level of society their capabilities allow them to. That's the theory, but the trouble with theories is that they work best on paper. You need certain infrastructures and systems in place to help people get along, and America would not appear to have those infrastructures in place, if you ask me. Our more enlightened neighbours in the Scandinavian countries have, however, realised the need for such support mechanisms, and the people there have accepted paying what we would consider punitive rates of income tax so that their countries can have a really effective social infrastructure, with good public health and welfare services. This, coupled with other things like the fact that the kids carry mobile phones to school instead of guns, has resulted in them being decidedly happier people, in a societal context, than their counterparts in the US.

So that's the money thing done there. Or not done I suppose, in that it's not part of the class for today, but I just wanted to explain why it wasn't. Now, on to Professor Layard's list in detail.

Mental health

Right, the mental health thing. This comes first on the list of factors affecting happiness, and rightly so, I suppose, because I think it's safe to say that if you were allowed to pick only one factor from the list that could be conferred on you for life, I reckon most people would go for mental health. Living in a country where access to a secure and satisfying job was guaranteed, the ratio of fabulous looking, sincere women with a great sense of humour and relatively little personal baggage was eight to one, the crime rate was near zero and you could leave your door unlocked at night, and the importance of personal freedom and a high level of moral values were entrenched in the psyche of the population would be of absolutely no use to you whatsoever if you were not of sound mind and in a position to seize the opportunities such a Utopian environment would afford you. Agreed? So when you next hear old people outside the church or farmers leaning on a stone wall saying, 'Ah but sure, your health is your wealth', listen to them, because they're right.

According to Mr Layard, Richard, no Dick, I'm sure Dick is fine, we're all friends here – I introduced him properly at the beginning. According to Dick, 'mental illness causes half of all the measured disability in our society and, even if you add in premature death, mental illness accounts for a quarter of the total impact of disease.' That's pretty mad, isn't it? Half of all measured disability in society. And in the UK, for example, only 12 per cent of the National Health Service budget is spent on mental illness, the shortsightedness of which is highlighted by the fact that 25 per cent of people experience serious mental illness at some point in their lives, and somewhere in the region of 15 per cent of us experience major depression. Many of the causes of such depression can be effectively treated or at least helped by a combination of drugs and various forms of therapy (cognitive therapy that is, as opposed to drug-them-up-to-their-eyeballs therapy), and yet only a quarter of the people suffering from depression are actually receiving treatment to help them.

If we agree to take Dick's percentages as being applicable to our situation, and I see no reason why we can't, that means that in Dublin alone, somewhere in the region of 150,000 people are suffering from depression, and 112,500 of them either don't know it yet or aren't receiving help for it, and worse still, a quarter of a million people in this city will experience mental illness at some point in their lives. I did try to get the corresponding percentage figure for what the Department of Health claims to spend on mental illness every year in Ireland as a proportion of its overall budget, but for one reason or another, I got no response to any of my numerous queries, one of which involved me being patched through to no less than eleven different extensions. I was only really looking for the figure for the sake of completeness; whatever it is, it couldn't possibly be enough, and this I know for a fact.

You see, I am quite possibly the world's worst patient – I hate being sick. I take it very personally, as though it's some kind of karmic payback for me breaking a red light or not letting somebody out in front of me at a busy junction. I can't stand even going to the doctor, and then going across the road with my prescription and then remembering to take the bloody tablets. I really hate hospitals. I hate the smell of them. I don't like the food. I don't like the enforced sure-we're-all-sick-so-let's-all-pretend-we're-the-best-of-friends groove you kind of have to get into with people you ordinarily wouldn't bother your arse talking to. I don't like people prodding at me and asking me questions. And I have a serious problem with some consultant hosting a John Bowman type Q&A session with a bunch of trainees, discussing the intimate details of my medical history for all to hear with an air of barely concealed dispassionate aloofness, who practises his golf swing as he leads his charges from ward to ward.

And the irony of this position is that over the past five years or so I have been in and out of more hospitals than most people ever will be, though not as a patient Thank God. Back in the day when I first started driving a taxi, the company I was renting the car from had loads of accounts with the Eastern Health Board and a number of the hospitals around town. It was only when I started driving a taxi that I discovered just how many hospitals there actually are in Dublin. And I always used to get a good laugh out of having a few nurses in the car on their way into town after a week of nights. They'd be going on about how exhausted they were and how hard the nights were, and how they needed the following week off to recuperate. And there was poor me, going straight from one week of nights into another week of nights with no week's paid leave in between. I used to keep my thoughts on the subject to myself, of course, but I changed my views about a year later after having been in and out of the Meath, James's, Tallaght, Our Lady's up in Crumlin, James Connolly Memorial in Blanchardstown, Beaumont, Clonskeagh, St Ita's out in

Portrane, St Loman's in Palmerstown, Holles Street, Temple Street, the Mater, Cherry Orchard, St Luke's in Rathgar, and the Rotunda, more times than I care to remember. The absolute shit that these medical personnel have to put up with as they try to go about their business is mind-boggling. I don't know how they do it, and am now firmly of the opinion that whatever amount of shit I had to contend with during any given week on the streets of Dublin, it probably didn't amount to a hill of beans when compared to the lot of a nurse facing into a week of nights, and that they fully deserve the following week off.

The hospital I dreaded going to the most was St Brendan's up in Grangegorman. If you weren't depressed going in there as a patient initially, you most certainly would be after a few days. The whole place had a *One-Flew-over-the-Cuckoo's-Nest* vibe to it. It was very eerie, like there was no way out once you went in through the big gates. Why you would locate a hospital dealing with such environmentally-influenced conditions like depression and homelessness in such a cold, dreary and unwelcoming place as this is quite beyond me. I am talking purely about the physical place here now, and not for one minute suggesting that the staff there did anything but the very best they could with what resources they had, which I could see straight off were both insufficient and strained, to say the least.

Some of the times that I would be transferring patients from one place to the other there would be a member of staff accompanying me. (On a purely financial level, this was sweet for me, because I would have to return them to wherever I picked them up from, so the fare would be hefty enough.) Most of the time though, it would be just me and the passenger concerned, which was pretty uncomfortable sometimes. I remember one time I was bringing a chap from St Brendan's out to St Loman's in Palmerstown. Poor sod was only about the same age as me, but looked at least ten years older. His eyes were glazed over and absent looking. Not from drugs, I didn't think, though; more an air of resignation that suggested he had become used to being shat on from on high for a long time now and was content to let himself be shuffled around from shelter to hostel to hospital like the surprise contents of a human pass-the-parcel game. He had all his worldly goods in a half filled black plastic refuse sack, and slumped into the front seat of the car with barely a sigh and half a nod of acknowledgement, apparently unaware of where we were going.

I was driving down the quays when all of a sudden he casually informed me that I could let him out at the next lights. I casually informed him that I couldn't actually do that – that our destination was Loman's in Palmerstown, and if he wanted to go elsewhere he'd have to make onward arrangements from Loman's. All of a sudden he flipped, started roaring and shouting at me, saying there was nothing wrong with him. Not long in the game, I wasn't really sure of what to do, so I got on the radio to the base and told them what was happening, in hindsight perhaps unkindly referring to my passenger as 'the patient'. Your man grabs the radio out of my hand and starts roaring into it at the base controller, telling them that he wasn't a patient and that there was nothing wrong with him. The base controller politely recommended that I proceed to Lucan with all necessary haste and ignore your man's pleas to stop the car. Thankfully, he calmed down a bit and I just kept him talking about anything and everything I could think of that didn't relate to the health services or his particular reason for being a passenger in my car. I get to Loman's eventually and pull up at the main reception. Your man gets quietly out of the car, thanking me politely as he goes and wanders into the building with a resigned, almost grateful look on him, as though, much as he doesn't want to be there, it's probably one of the few places where he feels he will get some degree of care, if only for a while until he gets bundled into another taxi to be shunted off somewhere else to make way for another unfortunate sod who can't get it together to make his own way in the city.

There are many, many professionals working in related areas who are infinitely better placed than I to comment on what is wrong with not just the health service as a whole, but with those units of the Department of Health that deal with provision of services to those suffering from mental illnesses. On a surface level, we all know that the health service is in a shambles, thanks partly to the nonsensical and archaic health board structures which appear to serve political needs more effectively than they do medical needs, and partly because of the overwhelming weight of the cumbersome administrative system that bears down on the medical personnel trying to do their jobs. With all the billions and billions of euros that have been poured into the Department of Health over the past number of years, only a minuscule proportion of these funds has been targeted at the area of mental health, and yet according to Professor Layard, problems associated with mental health account for half of the measured disabilities affecting our society.

That sobering figure on its own would surely suggest that

making a concerted effort to tackle this problem once and for all would contribute greatly to making our society a happier one.

Satisfying and secure work

Now, satisfying and secure work. I'm sure that most people would have a list of different factors that they would evaluate and score when asked if they felt satisfied with their job – pay and conditions, the commute, their working environment, the possibility of shagging a colleague, that sort of thing. But however much it may do your head in snailing along in poxy traffic to get to work, or however much it kills you to answer to a complete asshole, these factors would be given a lower weighting than actual job security, am I right?

Put it like this. However *satisfying* it would be to have your own dedicated traffic lane across the M50 or down the Stillorgan dual carriageway, a basement parking space beside an elevator that delivers you to your workstation, a Scarlett Johannson look-a-like across from you who has a secret crush on you and uses her fondness for giving full body massages as a way of getting close to you, a job that involves coming up with new ways of improving the aerodynamic qualities of swimsuits used exclusively by the Brazilian Olympic women's team which necessitates business class monthly visits to Rio to help them try on the newest creations, twelve week's annual leave on double pay, use of a vintage Aston Martin DB7 Vantage, a mid-six figure salary, no performance reviews and a Christmas party to beat all others, would you actually feel *secure* in that job if your contract was renewable every week, with no notice required should the company decide to up sticks and sod off to South Korea?

No, you wouldn't. Seriously, you wouldn't. But it might only last a week! And you see, if like most people in the world, your big picture lifetime goals would be something entirely commendable like, getting a good job, meeting somebody cool, settling down, buying a house, starting a family, all that kind of thing, well then job security has to come pretty much top of the list in terms of what factors you would actually cite when asked that big question about whether or not you were satisfied with your job, because those worthy goals are all fairly long-term ones, and you need to be able to plan a good way ahead to have any chance of attaining them.

I, on the other hand, being something of an asshole, don't aspire to any of those goals at all – apart from the meeting-somebody-cool one, but the chances of that happening are receding on an almost daily basis – and would therefore be able to categorically state that yes, I would find the dream job outlined above *entirely* satisfying, even if it only lasted one week. There are two reasons for this. The first is that, seeing as how I don't have an innate yearning to get married, buy a house, have kids and spend the rest of my life being told what to do by assholes who don't know what to do themselves, job security is not a priority for me, which is probably just as well given my current occupation as a professional writer. The second reason for me declaring that I would be totally satisfied with the Scarlett-Johannson-lookalike-masseuse-swimsuit-designing-Rio-visiting-Aston-Martin-driving-loads-of-cash-and-holidays job would be that a week spent in such a job would be infinitely better than the twelve months or so I spent working for two different companies since finishing college eleven years ago. Allow me to explain.

I started my short-lived corporate career working with Coca-Cola part time for a couple of years whilst in college. They had put up an ad in the canteen looking for merchandisers around May of one year. I saw the ad being posted by one of the hippies from the Student Union on a Monday morning, and displaying what I thought was a laudable degree of initiative, I promptly took it down as soon as he had gone back to munching his rice cakes and drawing up petitions. I rang the chap in Coca-Cola and confidently informed him that I was the man he was looking for and could start immediately after my bothersome exams were out of the way. And so I did – recruiting a pal of mine for them as well in the process – and not to put too fine a point on it, we kinda rocked. I know it's not an incredibly demanding job, stacking shelves with product conforming to a planogram pre-agreed at store level with all the labels facing out the same way, but all the same I don't know what kind of morons they had doing it before myself and Declan showed up on the scene, because they thought we were only great.

So anyway, the pair of us ended up going full time with them when we finished college, and believe it or not, we were two of the few people with jobs in the bag upon graduation. Jobs that today's shithead graduates wouldn't piss on too. We spent our days haring around the city getting as many calls as possible done, working fifty hours a week minimum, and all for £9,000 a year, the use of a commercial vehicle emblazoned with the Coca-Cola livery, plus all the carbonated piss you could drink. And that was only back in 1993.

My time with the company as a full-time employee was unexpectedly cut short though. As was my life, very nearly. I was seconded to the Galway office to work under this fat bastard who was trying to instil in the boys down there that there was a certain way of doing things, namely his way, or else, and all that hard ball kind of shit. So off I went to do my thing, experiencing the heady intoxicating buzz of 'towns' like Tuam, Ballina, Athenry, Westport and Killala. On the upside, my new vehicle was both livery-free and actually new as opposed to the hundred-thousand-mile old pieces of shit knocking around the Dublin depot.

My first week over, going in the opposite direction of all the culchies getting out of Dublin for the weekend, I hit the road to return home triumphantly. Not in my new vehicle, however. One of the Galway lads I was working with was off on a week's holiday the following week and wanted to swap vans with me, presumably so he could shag his girlfriend in the back of the van and not have any salacious reports of his antics getting back to Dough Boy in the office. Keen to get on the right side of my new colleagues I reluctantly agreed to the exchange and headed home in his noticeably under-powered piece of shit. Four years in college and look at me, maw, I'm on top o' the world. Well, on the N6 at any rate. Feeling a bit peckish at the halfway stage I stopped off in Rochfortbridge to get some munchies. As I got back into the van chomping on my Mars bar, almost as an afterthought, I decided to fasten my seatbelt.

Quite lucky too, really, because less than five minutes later and a couple of hundred yards up the road, I had a mad accident that nearly bloody killed me. I was stuck behind this forty foot and as the car in front of me pulled out to overtake, I did too. Your man in front got past the truck and slipped back in comfortably but in my poxy old van I was quickly running out of road to get past the bastard, and then before I knew what was going on, there were cars coming in the other direction straight at me. What to do? Couldn't get past him, couldn't get back in behind him because there were loads of cars there, so I pulled over on to the hard shoulder of the other side of the road and hit the brakes. Unfortunately, only a couple of seconds after hitting the brakes I then hit a post with one of those cat's eyes yokes on it. Well made yokes they are, too, because the van literally rebounded off the post and spun across the road, ending up in a ditch. I was grand, I have to say. Hopped out, not a scratch on me. A little dazed, which was understandable – I'd only been driving for a bloody week at the time. After surveying the wreckage I decided that there was little I could do in terms of rescuing the van. No mobile phones in those days, so I grabbed my bag and hitched a lift home.

I retuned to Galway that Sunday night to inform Dough Boy of my escapades, and needless to say, after making a token enquiry after my own condition, he let me know in no uncertain terms that things did not augur well for my future career with the company. I had kinda guessed as much myself. You see, Coca-Cola had so many vehicles of all descriptions on the road that they had their own internal driving test which everybody was supposed to sit before being handed the keys to one of the much-sought-after, logo-emblazoned commercial vehicles. My dispatch to

Galway had been something of a cloak and dagger affair though, with Dough Boy keen to have somebody he knew down there that he could manipulate easily (me, the hungry graduate looking for a break in the sales and marketing arena), as opposed to one of the lads in the Galway office getting the union involved so that he could parachute his third cousin from two-mile out the Ballygar road into the vacant position where he could sit on his arse for the rest of his life. In his haste to get me down there to act as his personal gimp, he had neglected to ensure that I first sit the internal driving test, and once the insurance company heard about this, it was sayonara Tuam for Do. Haven't eaten a Mars bar since either.

To say my tail was between my legs as I made the return journey home would be something of an understatement. It was a defining moment in my life, though, and as I rattled towards Dublin aboard a rattly old Bus Éireann coach, I formulated my comeback plan, calling, for the first of many times, on my heretofore untapped reserves of personal resilience. I promptly spruced up my CV and lashed it off to a few recruitment agencies, obviously neglecting to recount the terms of my decidedly inglorious departure from Coca-Cola, and expounding somewhat on both my length of service to the company and the duties I had undertaken during my time there.

Sure enough, I got another job a few months later. Same kind of thing really – I became a van sales representative for Van den Bergh Foods. No, I had never heard of them either, but they were the crowd behind HB, Bird's Eye and McDonnell's, so they were big enough. They had decided to make an assault on the Irish tea market, hoping to give

Lyon's and Barry's a run for their money, but after holing us up in some hotel in Portlaoise for two days to listen to successive morons outline their sales and marketing strategies, I have to say I didn't fancy their chances at all. I decided to keep this to myself for the time being and see how thing went.

Before I get to the gory details of my glorious exit from the company some six months later, I just have to tell you a little story about my first day reporting for duty. (A sub-story, I suppose you could call it, in that I'm already telling you a story.) We were told to assemble at HQ at nine o'clock on the Monday morning which, handily enough for me, was only ten-minutes walk from my folks' house. I strolled down early enough to suss out the competition, which weren't hard to spot, bedecked as we all were in our corporate uniforms – itchy, grey, secondary school type trousers, lemon yellow polyester shirts, cheapo green blazers with the Lipton logo on the breast pocket, and a narrow wine tie, again emblazoned with the Lipton logo, just in case it didn't hit you in the face the first time. Lemon yellow regulation issue jocks too. Ah no, only messing – the trousers weren't that itchy.

As I walked past the security hut towards the offices I was positively accosted by another of the sales reps. He introduced himself to me in this dementedly excited voice as though we were about to embark on the adventure of a lifetime. Best foot forward and all that, but it was half eight on a Monday morning, for God's sake. I smiled politely, introduced myself and let him prattle on about all the high-powered execs we would be reporting to. He continued with a list the length of your arm of people to watch out for, which didn't bode well for the interpersonal side of things, I felt. (He had also neglected to include himself on that same list so I immediately suspected him to be a sly kind of nutter.)

No less than a minute later he was, however, the source of one of the funniest incidents I have ever encountered. Pure situation comedy. It probably won't sound as funny to you now because you weren't there, but trust me, I still piss myself every time I think of it. We were sitting in the lobby of the offices waiting to be ushered into the boardroom for our final bullshit motivational speeches from the great and the good before going forth to conquer the Irish tea market. Rather, *I* was sitting down comfortably. Head the ball was standing, even though there were ample seats. (I hate people who stand up when there are seats available. Why? Take a load off. It's normally a function of their insecurity, I reckon. They want to see everything that's happening around them, and to be seen and heard by all around them too. Particularly if they are short in stature too, I find, which is most perplexing.) Your man was still yakking on, listing in great detail the numerous companies involved in the Van den Bergh empire, and how we fitted into the overall picture of things.

'So, ye see, even tho' wear an independent operation, wear still under de *auspicious* of Van den Bearg at de end o' de day,' he says to me, wrapping up his lengthy explanation of the webbed ownership structure of one of Europe's largest consumer goods conglomerates.

Auspicious? Surely, he meant *auspices*? Or maybe I just heard him incorrectly. It was only a quarter to nine after all, and mornings aren't my forte.

'How do you mean exactly?' I asked in a confused tone, mostly to stop myself from laughing, but also to give him a chance to correct himself.

'Well, wear here, righ'?' he explained once again, sighing somewhat as he gestured around with his hands, helpfully confirming to me that I wasn't actually having an out-of-body experience. 'And Van den Bearg, dey're here, righ'?' he continues, pointing upwards with his right hand. 'An' all in here ye have de rest o' de companies, yeah? Yer Bird's Eye, yer HB, yer McDonnell's an' all dat, yeah? So wen wear out dere doin' our ting, we have de Van den Bearg name goin' fer is, d'ye see? The Lipton operation is under deir auspicious.'

No, there it was again. Auspicious. He definitely said auspicious. Gonna have to watch this fella.

'Ah yeah, now I have you, right,' I answered, making a mental note to do all I could to avoid talking to him ever again.

Anyway, that's how the first day in the new job started. Not very encouraging, I think you'll agree. And from there, things got steadily worse. Turned out 'Auspicious', as I had now privately christened him, was on my bloody sales team, and I would see him first thing every shagging morning. Not only that, the goons supervising us had no idea what they were doing. The tea category was like an alien universe to them, it was so far removed from – in their eyes at any rate – the comfortable world of Golly Bars and frozen chicken drumsticks. After the first two weeks, I knew we were on a hiding to nothing, and confided as much in one of the other lads on my team. His sceptical looks and raised eyebrows whenever easily achieved sales targets and lucrative commission payments were mentioned singled him out to me as someone with a brain, and sure enough, he too reckoned it was a lost cause even at this early stage.

I soldiered on for a couple of months, kept the head down – went out every day on my calls, had a nap in the van in the car park of Quinnsworth's in Greystones; drove back to the base the long way over the mountains. Killing time really. Then one day I spotted an ad for a job in the McDonnell's side of things. Same kind of job, but higher basic salary, a car-van instead of a poxy Transit van, selling established products, not some shitty US import nobody wanted to know about, and best of all, the people running the show were totally removed from the clowns I had the misfortune to be lumbered with at the time. (McDonnell's, as with Lipton, was of course still under the 'auspicious' of Van den Bergh.) I applied straight away and progressed swiftly to the second round of interviews, which were held in the Royal Marine Hotel in Dún Laoghaire.

I sauntered in and got on great with the two boys there. As the interview was wrapping up they asked to me to go over to the window of the conference room, which was on the second floor, I think, put myself in the shoes of the manager of that particular hotel, have a good look around and tell them what I thought. Bit odd, but fair play, I applauded their thinking-outside-the-box vibe. I strolled over to the window and had a good look around, scanning as far and wide as my eyes could see, knowing that my answer to their question could release me from the lemon yellow hell I was currently trapped in. Nothing out of the ordinary struck me straight away, I have to say, and just as I was about to return to my seat and trot out some clichéd shit about having a bird's eye view on things (no pun intended), I noticed something down at basement level. There was an alleyway running right around the basement of the hotel, and from this room, and all other guest rooms, I concluded, you could see no end of shit just thrown there. Pallets, boxes, trolleys, refuse sacks, you name it, it was like a bomb hit it. Bingo. Had it. I strolled casually back to my seat and sat down. I told the two boys that if I were the manager of the hotel and saw that mess down there I would firstly, obviously, get it cleaned up. Secondly, and more importantly, it would cause me to re-evaluate all other aspects of the running of the hotel, operations and procedures you might think are dandy on the surface but which reveal themselves to be seriously flawed upon closer examination, no time for complacency, all that kind of stuff. The boys were loving it, nodding their heads and smiling away. They welcomed me aboard and I split back to the base with a smile on my face.

A few days later I was called up to see one of the sales managers. He wasn't keen at all on my lateral move, in that it reflected badly on his ability to motivate and retain personnel. I said it just wasn't working out the way I had thought it would and had decided to move on, etc etc. Do you know what the moron did? Vetoed my move across to the McDonnell's side of things. Complete tosser. I said nothing, just planned my speedy exit from the company as a whole. When the time came to nominate our preferred weeks for the summer holidays, I took the earliest available slot, and opted for three weeks instead of two. Holiday commission was calculated as an average of the previous two weeks' sales or something like that, I can't remember. What

I can remember, though, is that for the month before I went away I loaded up every single outlet on my route with as much tea as I possibly could, lashing it in everywhere, giving them enough of the shit to see them through for the next two years at the rate it was selling. Then, as soon as I got my hefty three week's holiday pay, I handed in my letter of resignation, vowing to never work for anyone again as long as I lived.

(I managed to keep up that vow until February 2001 when my fiscal situation was so abhorrent after the calamitous movie production episode that I had to get a job for a while. I deliberately took a handy enough number with zero prospects or responsibility, delivering office supplies. My colleagues were all sound enough – as with a lot of companies, it was the tossers who owned the operation that were complete knobs. I jacked it in a couple of months later and have since re-sworn my vows.)

So that's my potted history of being employed, as opposed to self-employed. Didn't really pan out as I had initially expected, but looking back on it now, coming across all those morons was the best thing that ever happened to me. Since those dark days, I have tried my hand at a fair few things and have always managed to make a dollar from them and am confident that I will never be unable to put bread on my own little table. As an ex-merchandiser, ex-van sales representative, ex-bread distribution agent, ex-courier, ex-office products delivery person, ex-Blackrock market crepe vendor, ex-film producer, ex-taxi driver, and soon-to-be-ex-writer-if-this-sodding-book-doesn't-sell, I have now finally reached the stage where I am positively unemployable. A quick glance at my 'CV' would scare the shit out of most employers, firstly because they would recognise – quite rightly – that I would be gone out the door as soon as something more interesting presented itself, and that secondly, I would probably be in a position to do their job better than they are currently doing it, and if there is one thing a 'superior' doesn't want it's an underling they know is better able to their job than they are.

Anyway, Dick's list rightly stipulates 'secure *and* satisfying' work, because the two go hand in hand. If people feel they enjoy a good degree of job security, they will, for the most part I think, work hard and derive some satisfaction from their job, however menial it is. And, if companies make it their business to ensure their staff are satisfied in their place of work, they will be rewarded with greater productivity and loyalty, to such an extent even, that if a decision was made to look at the option of shifting production to a lower-cost environment like South Korea, the quantifiable benefits of high workforce morale and productivity could outweigh the savings to be made with more traditional business costs like rent and rates that such a move would generate.

And it doesn't take a whole lot to make people happy at work really – pay them a fair wage, treat them with respect, and empower them to recognise that they can achieve something. And do something nice every now and then, doesn't have to be anything huge, just something that lets them know you appreciate their efforts. For instance, I remember a couple of years ago some radio show asked people to ring in and tell them about how nice their boss was, if they were lucky enough to be working for a decent sort of chap. Loads of people rang in, of course, telling all sorts of stories, half of which were probably bullshit tales told to try and win the shitty prize of a couple of cinema passes, but one that stuck in my mind was from a gang who worked for an equipment hire company called Elevation, based down in Hazelhatch, Co. Kildare. Every Friday their boss would get pizzas delivered for lunch for all the staff and then disappear off home or to the golf course shortly afterwards, and it was kind of an unwritten rule that everybody else could sod off home as well once they had cleared their desk as it were, of both pizza crumbs and business-related matters. Kinda cool isn't it? Sound bloke. Hope he's still doing it.

At the other extreme of this progressive management style is the MD of a company I won't bother naming. Last Christmas I had to collect four girls from this particular company's offices up in Rathfarnham. They were off into town for their work do, and it turned out that they had to organise and pay for it themselves because the MD had told them that business wasn't great that year, money was tight, and belts were going to have be fastened, all that kind of shit. And do you know what he did? Went off with his fellow directors for a slap-up meal in a swanky restaurant without saying a word. What an asshole. To my mind, the best thing he could have done was to make the announcement about business being bad and not having had such a good year – if it was true of course – and then brought them all out for the meal and a few drinks anyway, to show his appreciation for their efforts over same not so good year. I'm sure that whatever it cost him would have been more than offset by the half a dozen spoof sickies which were no doubt pulled by staff the following year, quite rightly figurng that if he didn't give a toss about them they couldn't give a toss about him.

So, having said all that, how does Ireland fare in the secure and satisfying stakes? Well, unfortunately, I didn't have time to compile a comprehensive questionnaire and survey a representative sample of the Irish workforce to assess their views on the subject, so I'm not going to say a whole lot definitively on the subject. I don't want that to come across as a cop-out, it's just that to answer the question with any kind of certainty would necessitate the regurgitation of any number of reports from the ESRI and others I slagged off in the prologue, and most of you'd end up skipping the few pages anyway, so why bother? I'll leave it for you to answer for yourselves.

What I will say about job security is that it doesn't appear to be a given in globalised, modern Ireland the way it used to be – to some extent at least – where people finished school or college, got a job and pretty much stuck at it unless circumstances dictated otherwise. These days, people in the job market are required to have a fair amount of resilience and adaptability, as companies continually seek to tip the scales ever further in their favour in terms of flexibility and responsiveness, upsizing quickly at the first sight of a tiger cub's pubescent development and then downsizing again even quicker as soon as the mature tiger begins to slow down. That's all part of the economic cycle, I know, but would surely indicate, even on an admittedly basic kind of level, that nowadays a job itself certainly doesn't come with job security attached.

When the IDA and similar agencies were established, the jobs created by the companies they lured here were by and large new jobs. Real new jobs, in that a lot of the people who took up employment with these companies were either previously unemployed or maybe working in a family agricultural concern that wasn't really generating an income for them. So if a midlands town got a new factory employing 68 people, that was 68 new jobs and 68 new wage packets in circulation. Nowadays though, with every other European country, quite rightly, looking to increase its standard of living, the competition to secure these new jobs is intense. Also, every year, many foreign-owned companies shift production to an emerging economic region where the payroll costs are a fraction of what they are here, resulting in thousands of job losses. The effect of this is that the IDA and other state agencies like them are left playing catch up to some degree in that now when a midlands town gets a new factory with 68 'new' jobs, chances are they may not be new jobs at all, but replacements for the 68 jobs that were lost the previous year with the closure of a textile factory.

There is also a growing tendency for companies to push highly flexible contracts on new recruits, particularly in relation to low-skilled jobs. Many of the people who would be taking up these jobs may be people returning to the workforce for the first time in a good number of years, maybe as a result of a period of long-term unemployment or family responsibilities, or people from less privileged areas of society where opportunities for further education were severely limited and in some cases discouraged in favour of getting a job – any job – that would contribute to the household income, and I would think that what they would most value in their new job would be an element of security, not a zero hours contract being thrust at them on day one, but that's the way things are going.

In years gone by, when things weren't half as good as they are now – in an economic sense – job security was not the issue it is these days, when we are all apparently richer. This is partly explained by the fact that whatever about before, nowadays the structure of the working environment in which the majority of the population is caught up is controlled by a relatively small number of people whose primary aim is to keep it that way, thereby creating even more wealth for themselves and their related stakeholders. However regrettable it is that such a comparatively small number of people can effectively control the lives and by extension the long-term aspirations of so many people – property ownership, starting a family etc. – this is the way things work under the classical economic models that have been pursued by first and second world administrations for decades, and the validation of such an approach, when compared coldly to the communist model, for example, cannot be disputed in purely economic terms. (Funny thing is though, that in what's left of Russia today, with 30 per cent of the population living in poverty under Putin's allegedly reformist Western-influenced leadership, millions of elderly people hanker after the old communist days, an era which they remember as being more equitable.)

The migration to open economy inevitably results in a significant increase in the level of economic activity in a country. The main obstacle to ensuring that everybody in society actually benefits from this increased activity is one of redistribution. We live in a knowledge economy, which at its simplest and most logical level means that if you're smart, you get on, and if you're not, you'll get left behind. You can be clever-Dick-smart and get ahead on brain power alone, or you can be street-smart and get ahead by spotting opportunities and exploiting them. Either way, an education is critical. The small element who get richer and richer as a result of increased wealth on a national level don't really give a shit about anyone else – they know no better, they were born into certain circumstances and grow up in that cosseted environment. The larger element of society that basically works, not so much for a living anymore, but for a life, manage somehow to extract some satisfaction and pleasure from outside their work day which makes the following work day tolerable and instrumental in achieving a more personal goal of some description. There remains a large group of people, though, who for a number of reasons, the main one being their inability to secure an adequate education, never reach the stage where they too can enjoy the benefits economic expansion brings. And unfortunately, the gap between this group of people and the rest of society is widening on an annual basis.

A purely economic, quantitative analysis of the 'progress' of a particular country takes no account of how happy the people in that country may be. One near certainty, though, is that the majority of the people of that country, outside of the group who control the wealth associated with the economic development of the country, are becoming more vulnerable to arriving at a state of distinct *un*happiness as the issue of job security becomes less and less of a given.

Jesus, I'm knackered after that. Thought I'd written about ten pages there instead of a couple of poxy paragraphs. So, as for job satisfaction? Sod it, maybe you should put a note in the suggestion box at work putting forward the free-pizza-and-piss-off-home-early-on-a-Friday idea and see how it goes down.

A secure and loving private life

Next up is a secure and loving private life. I suppose it's fairly obvious that such a factor would be crucial in assessing the level of everybody's happiness index, given the strength of people's need for companionship and all that, but as you will have learned from the little story I opened this chapter with and the whole Copenhagen thing last December, those cumulative three months or so being the sum total of my 'relationship history' over the past four years, the highs and lows of a secure and loving private life are not something I personally have a whole lot of experience of. But all the same, whilst acknowledging that what works for two particular people (or three if that's your thing) may not work for two (or three) other people, from the little I have learned of such matters firsthand, and the lot I have seen of such matters second-hand in the confines of my taxi, I would have thought that there were a few universal givens on what constitutes a secure and loving private life.

The first of these would be that it's just that – a *private* life. Something to be nourished and enjoyed between two people only, and not two people and whoever else they can foist the details of their relationship on. I can't stand people who feel that everybody they come across is as interested in the details of their love lives as they are. I've often been told – not always in a flattering way I might add – that I have a remarkable ability to convey an air of intense disinterest and/or disdain to people when they're spouting any sort of rubbish in my general direction. It's something I've worked hard to perfect over the years, and have found it invaluable in my dealings with the public at large, and particularly with the public at small in the back of my taxi. However, when the topic of conversation has veered towards the area of personal relationships, my powers of conveyance didn't seem to do the trick at all.

People seemed to look on me as some kind of counsellor; it was as if the paltry fare I was receiving for the trip was inclusive of some kind of feel-free-to-wreck-my-head-with-every-last-nuance-of-your-current-realtionship surcharge. Regrettable as it was that I had come across them in the first place, it was highly unlikely that I would ever see them again. I didn't go to school with them, I didn't grow up with them, I didn't work with them or socialise with them, so what possible interest could I have in the state of their love life? And yet he/she would persist, asking me what I thought he/she should do in light of the most recent tiff that had stalled the otherwise smooth progress he/she was allegedly making.

The only thing excusing their relentless babbling was that they were invariably pissed when harassing me so. (This was in fact the prime reason I avoided chit chat with people at all unless I thought they were interesting in some way and might have a good story to tell me, in that any pearls of wisdom I deigned to impart would be forgotten by the time they had turned the key in the door.) Were they sober and asked themselves these same questions in the privacy of their own bedrooms the answer would have been blindingly obvious. The he and she concerned were totally unsuited to each other, and the relationship under scrutiny was fundamentally unhealthy and doomed to failure at some point in the future.

The next given that I would suggest in an integral constituent of a secure and loving private life is the whole compatibility thing. Whatever about different strokes for different folks and all that, and however easily a lot of us could overlook some serious character flaws in the short term if the sex was great, I'm sure we're all in agreement that at least a basic level of compatibility is a prerequisite for a sustainable relationship. So why is it that so many people get involved with people they just aren't suited to? I know that some people inexplicably thrive on drama, others are just so insecure that they would go out with any old gobshite rather than stay single, and most bizarrely, others still will quite openly and soberly profess that 'making up is just *so* great'. But even discounting morons of such persuasions, there are still thousands of people out there going out with people they really shouldn't be. And if I can see it in the space of ten minutes, why can't they, when the idiots spend day after day and night after night with each other? I must also add that it is invariably women who are at fault here, in that for whatever reason, they continually allow themselves to be strung along by the most boorish, insincere, pathologically lying assholes on the face of the earth.

I had this couple in the car one night, got them off the rank on the Green. I was raging because they were only going as far as The Mercantile on bloody Dame Street. Don't know why they couldn't have just walked down Grafton Street instead of dragging me away from pole position for less than a poxy fiver, but there you go. Big deep sigh and away we go. Half way down Dawson Street your man starts yawning and saying that he's tired and might go on home. She's all upset about him not coming in to meet her friends from work (why exactly I couldn't figure out, he wasn't up to much), and then he starts moaning on about how much shit he had on at work the next day, trying to make her feel bad. I wasn't even looking at him and I could tell he was lying, but then she's all apologies and starts in with the fingers-through-his-receding-hair thing and everything's hunky dory again. I stop outside The Mercantile and after a bit of slobbering she gets out. The door wasn't closed and your man was on the mobile to his mates enquiring if the do they were at was still on the go. Delighted to hear it was he quickly tells me to head down towards Baggot Street to Searson's before continuing his conversation with his buddies, decidedly perkier than he was thirty seconds previously.

Even more bizarrely, with a city full of assholes like that guy and misguided women content to go out with them, there seems to be no let-up in the number of weddings taking place every year, with thousands of people swearing their undying love and fidelity to each other. (I was going to do up a little chart showing the actual number of marriages every year for the past five years and then compute a rolling average, but the relevant information wasn't easily obtainable, and with time pressing on you'll have to settle for 'thousands', which is, I'm sure you'll agree, a fairly accurate guesstimate.) In 2003, for example, I was at *three* weddings. Now for someone as unsociable as myself, that's quite a tally. (And I was present at these weddings as a pivotal guest, integral to the proceedings and everyone's enjoyment of the day out, not as some 'plus one' hanger-on.) And all these weddings had been planned months in advance so as to secure the desired venue and date. I'm sure the weddings I attended will all work out dandy enough, but the same surely can't be said for every nuptial blessing that takes place the length and breadth of the country every year.

I suppose at the end of the day, people simply refuse to see what they don't want to see, however naïve that is, particularly in the long term. I've come across people like this three thousand six hundred and forty seven times (that is an accurate figure by the way – I maintained meticulous records from my time on the mean streets), and I can see the regret in their faces or hear it in their exchanges with their partners. I just know that they know they've made a mistake, but for whatever reason, they just soldier on. Could be out of consideration for the kids that may be in the equation, or maybe the whole money thing, paying alimony and child support, two mortgages and all that, or maybe, quite simply, it could be a case of better the devil you know. Whatever it is, it wouldn't work for me; I know that. In all honesty, I probably wouldn't work for too many women out there either, but at least I can recognise and acknowledge that and just make a mess of one life as opposed to two.

Having said that, the divorce thing is of course on the table now, an innovation not afforded to our elders in times past. Since its long overdue introduction a few years ago, many, many people have filed for divorce in Ireland. (I don't have the exact figures to hand – made a few calls to try and find out, but no joy. I'd say it's a lot, though, which equates roughly to 'many, many'.) It's not necessarily a reflection of some greater malaise affecting Irish society, I don't think, just a belated confirmation that a lot of people aren't happy with the life partner choices they made years ago and want either a second chance or just a clean break from the misery they find themselves trapped in.

There are people – mostly old people narked they didn't have the option themselves – who say that the advent of divorce in Ireland has made it all too easy for people to bail out of a difficult situation and that people aren't prepared to 'work' at relationships anymore. Personally, however reluctant I am to work in general, the one thing I was definitely never prepared to work at was relationships. I thought that was the whole idea, to be honest with you. You meet somebody cool, she's happy with the way you are, you're happy with the way she is, you can both handle a couple of little idiosyncrasies in each other's character without silently vowing the week before you get married to make it your life's work to eradicate such idiosyncrasies from the other, accepting that it's the good and the bad in the person that makes them the person they are and the person you fell for, and you live happily ever after. From where I'm standing, that ain't work, that's sweet.

It's like a packet of Revels – yum, yum. Apart from the coffee ones: I think they're gak. But I have to accept that there's gonna be a couple of them in there and getting caught out with one or two of them isn't going to ruin the satisfaction I get from the rest of the packet. (My own research would indicate an average of 1.87 coffee-flavoured Revels per 35g packet. Unfortunately, time constraints didn't facilitate me researching the larger packets retailed in cinemas and supermarkets, so I'm not in a position to give you an across-the-range cumulative average.) It's an all or nothing thing, you see – they're not gonna do a special coffee-free production run just for me (as I have been informed on no fewer than five occasions, the last time quite emphatically). In fact, there are probably loads of sickos out there who would consider the coffee ones to be their favourites. And that's the thing – what works for me may not work for you, and vice versa. And so, if I was lucky enough to meet a cool chick who was pretty much everything I was looking for, possessed of only a couple of minor character flaws, and she was somehow bizarrely attracted to what I had to offer, I sure as shit wouldn't waste valuable time chipping away trying to erase those minor blemishes from her personality.

I'm just after realising that there is a possibility that my highly illuminating Revels truism could be interpreted in much the same way as that moron Forrest Gump's pathetic 'Life's like a box of chocolates; you don't know what's on the inside' pearl of wisdom from the abysmal movie of the same name. That would be a grave mistake on your part, for two reasons. Firstly, as I have just alluded to but wish to reiterate, Forrest Gump is a shit movie, partly because Tom Hanks is in it, but mostly because it celebrates naïvety and stupidity. Secondly, Forrest's 'words of wisdom' are in fact fundamentally flawed, in that by taking a moment to study the little menu inside the box, provided at some cost by the manufacturer, and for a specific reason, you *do* know what's inside the chocolates before you eat them, and can therefore avoid the ones with fillings not to your liking. The same cannot be said for a pack of Revels, however. There is no similar menu, either inside the packet or printed on the packaging itself, to help guide you through the assortment, so apart from the Minstrels and Maltesers ones, distinguishable respectively by their disc-like and comparatively larger shape, eating a packet of Revels really is something of a venture into the unknown. Just like relationships and marriage.

Whilst many would consider divorce to be the bluntest tool in the marriage guidance/counselling arsenal, I think it's very important that it not be considered in so harsh a light. Nobody has a crystal ball and things don't always work out the way you thought they would. So if you marry a guy/girl and a couple of years down the line they turn out to be the *de facto* asshole/bitch your mother/mates told you they were before you married them, at least now you can get out of it, salvage your freedom, start again and make something out of the rest of your life. Wallowing in misery achieves nothing.

Another given as far as the whole secure/loving private life thing goes (as far as I'm concerned anyway), is the sharing of similar aspirations. Again, that may sound fairly obvious, but all the same it never ceases to amaze me how or why so many people with wildly differing views on what they want out of life get together in the first place. And it's not the same as the compatibility thing, which now that I think about it I should maybe have called 'personal' compatibility, to distinguish it from 'life' compatibility, which is what I'm referring to here with the shared goals and aspirations thing. You see, it's one thing finding your soul mate on a personal level where you both have the same sense of humour or no sense of humour at all, are both staunch vegans or lusty carnivores, both love animals or fully support their continued use in chemical trials, both despise children or think they really are the future, both like it wild and adventurous or tender and loving, both think the city is totally where it's at or that there's nothing like the country life, both enjoy a line of coke before going out on the tear or think drugs of all classes are a scourge on society, both agree that cooking is a complete waste of time or that it's as good as foreplay gets, all that kind of stuff, but it's quite another to find that you both want to incorporate all of these things into the same kind of life.

Back to my example at the start of this chapter – I met this totally cool chick, we had a lot in common, particularly in terms of the fundamentals, but what she wanted out of her life at that point in time was not the same as what I wanted: her. However well we got on together, the timing wasn't right for her. Or maybe I was just delusional all along, and she was never that interested in me anyway, but you get the idea. If you're a happy-go-lucky sort of individual who isn't totally caught up in the corporate rat race and suburban mediocrity that goes with it and you meet some cool girl/guy that you get on really well with and have a great laugh with who *is* caught up in all that shit and thinks it's great, then I don't think that's a banker of a relationship. Somewhere down the line, your differing views on what life's all about are going to put serious pressure on how you see your future together, or don't see it together, more likely. So why invest considerable time and energy in a relationship that can't go full term?

Ultimately, given what I am told is an unorthodox position on these matters, I suppose I have to concede that

I don't have any hard and fast answers on the whole relationship thing that are going to find favour with the vast majority of you, so I think I'll leave it there. Whatever rocks your world.

A safe community

Gardaí today appealed for help into discovering what happened to a 57-year-old man who was found unconscious in Baggot Street. The man was found between 2.30am and 3am on Sunday morning and was swiftly rushed to St Vincent's Hospital, where he has remained unconscious.

Two teenage girls described as thugs have been detained after they were convicted for violently mugging other teenagers. In one of the incidents a young girl was held from behind with an arm across her neck before she was thrown and pinned to the ground by one of her muggers. As she was held down, the second mugger rifled through her pockets and made off with her mobile phone. In another incident an hour later one of the two girls approached a young woman and used force as she tried to rob her handbag. She then slapped the woman across the face.

A man appeared in Dublin District Court yesterday charged with the murder of a man in a Temple Bar pub on Tuesday night.

A 20-year-old man has been jailed for five years for raping a young girl in an incident involving what Mr Justice Kearns described as an element of collusion by her friends. James O'Donoghue of Mallow Road, Cork, was found guilty by a

Central Criminal Court jury last September of abducting and raping the then 13-year-old girl on 3 August 2001, in Tipperary. He was 16 when he committed the offences.

A 14-year-old boy along with three other teenagers and a 24-year-old man were last night charged with the rape of a woman in her thirties at Cratloe Wood, Co. Clare, in the early hours of yesterday. The five are also charged with the false imprisonment of the woman's partner contrary to Section 15 of the Non-Fatal Offences Against the Person Act at Cratloe yesterday. They are facing a separate charge of stealing car-keys, a wallet and a mobile phone worth €250 from the same man.

A frantic 999 call made by the girlfriend of a man killed during a row with his father was played for a murder trial jury at the Central Criminal Court yesterday.

The above snippets, culled from a random selection of newspapers over a short period of time, bear testament to the fact that we do not live in a safe community, the fourth factor influencing our level of happiness. Before I started to write this section, I took myself off to the Government Publications Office to get a copy of some reports which might have contained some useful facts and figures that I could use. Sad thing was, the most recent crime figures available for my perusal last month, March 2004, related to the year 2002. How pathetic is that? What relevance do they have some fifteen months later? Flicking through the few reports available on related issues didn't enlighten me to a huge degree anyway. As the man said, 'There are lies, damn lies, and then there's statistics.'

You see, statistics can always be used to one's advantage, depending on who one is and what one would rather deflect scrutiny away from and draw favourable attention to. So if a particular crime category showed a huge increase on the previous year and wouldn't make for pleasant reading in the run-up to the local elections or the assumption of the EU presidency, then one could simply split the old category into two or more new categories or sub-categories, therefore rendering direct year-on-year comparisons impractical and inaccurate. We all do it at one time or another, I suppose. 'Yeah, I know I failed Maths, mum, but why focus on the top line results only? Look at my B+ for Advanced Basketwork, what does that tell you?' That kind of thing.

Anyway, in the report, it states that there were 52 murders in the state in 2002. This figure is exactly the same as the corresponding figure for 2001, suggesting that the assassin-for-hire business is flat, failing to keep pace with other growth areas of the booming crime sector, such as armed robberies, an area of frantic activity which is obviously attracting the smart money, with reported incidents up an impressive 66 per cent on the previous year. And so, as is the case with all government propaganda, there are a couple of anomalies in the report worthy of mention. As I said, there were 52 murders in the state last year. The number of 'homicide cases' investigated was 133, significantly up from the 2001 figure of 74. Despite what the term might suggest to morons like you and me, a 'homicide case' does not in fact concern itself with murder *per se*. Homicide cases concern themselves with man-slaughter, attempted murder and reported murder threats. Well, that's alright then, isn't it? Manslaughter is the crime of killing a human being without the malice aforethought required for it to be classed as murder, so this would be the case if you stabbed your boyfriend to death on the spur of the moment with a kitchen knife after catching him shagging your sister, or repeatedly kicked the face off some guy who dared admire your girlfriend's arse in a nightlclub, leaving him to die in a lane near the Liffey, that sort of thing. Nothing to be concerned about, really; it's not murder. And then there's attempted murder, where the perpetrator didn't actually succeed in his mission to murder another person – that doesn't really count because of the perpetrator's ineptness. And as for threatening to murder someone, well that might just as well be described as tomfoolery, I suppose, nothing too serious.

The annual figures for 2002 also show that the number of rape cases reported was up by 25 per cent. Physical assaults causing injury were up by more than 60 per cent, though it doesn't break this figure down to show the number of Gardaí against whom reports of physical assaults were made, which I thought would have been both progressive and illuminating.

One thing to remember about statistics such as these which are issued by the Gardaí is that they tell us just one part of the story about the crime scene in Ireland. This is because they relate to reported crimes only. And that's fair enough: however long it takes them to do it, the cops can only release figures on crimes that are actually reported to them. The other, more interesting part of the story about the crime story in Ireland is to be found in the number of crimes carried out that *aren't* reported. And a survey conducted earlier this year revealed that this figure is as high as 20 per cent, and as high as 33 per cent for crimes suffered by those aged under 25. The reason for this high level of unreported crime is, for the most part, down to the undeniable fall-off in public confidence in the Gardaí in recent years. And the reasons for this fall-off in confidence in the Gardaí no doubt stems to some degree from the bad press it has deservedly received in relation to a number of high-profile incidents, such as the McBrearty affair in Donegal, the fatal shooting of John Carthy in Longford, and the excessive force used by some members of the force whilst trying to contain the highly agitated protestors taking part in the May Day parade. However it came about, one thing is certain: a large proportion of the general public are now of the opinion that the Gardaí either don't particularly care about the crime levels, or don't have the professional competence to get a result, and consequently people don't report the crime in question. The unfortunate knock-on effect of this decision is that it reinforces the air of invincibility that seems to be characteristic of so many scumbags on the streets nowadays, who go about their business of preying on innocent people with an alarming level of confidence.

Another thing that has to be considered when discussing the public's lack of confidence in the Gardaí is the Gardaí's own apparent feelings of invincibility when it comes to them being accused of wrongdoing of some description. On my little shopping trip into the Government Publications Office, I also bought a copy of the Garda Síochána Complaints Board annual report. Again, however pathetic it is, the most recent one available was for the year 2002, having only been released in December 2003. And the spin the Board managed to put on some of the matters before them is hilarious, really. For instance, commenting on the 'Reclaim the Streets' protest in May which led to 41 separate complaints to the Board from members of the public, Gordon Holmes, the Chairman, when commenting on the fact that he and his colleagues had to contend with a record number of complaints for 2002, says: 'The Board's firm action on the "Reclaim the Streets" march issue has also restored a good deal of confidence in it. This is shown by the fact that the Board has received more complaints this year than ever before.'

Isn't that gas? Receiving a record number of complaints – 1,405 in all, up 10 per cent on the previous year, 750 of which relate to the six divisions comprising the Dublin Metropolitan Area – is not something to be proud of, I wouldn't have thought, but there you go. More ridiculously still, get this. The Board has to request the Garda Commissioner to appoint a separate investigating officer into every single complaint made against one of our boys in blue. Up North, where admittedly they may have more reason than we do to be making complaints against the cops, the equivalent body doesn't have to go knocking on the super's door to ask permission to do their job, they can just waltz in unannounced to a police station at any time and seize any and all documentation they feel may be of help to them in their investigations.

Any degree of scrutiny of this annual report would suggest that it operates at a level well below that which is required in order for the public to have any confidence in it whatsoever. At the start of its year, the Board was currently dealing with 792 complaints. It reopened 17 old cases and received 1,405 new complaints, giving it 2,214 cases to consider on an initial level. The number of complaints withdrawn, not proceeded with or deemed inadmissible by the Chief Executive totalled 684, leaving 1,530 complaints requiring the Board's attention; 214 of these were either later withdrawn or not proceeded with, and a further 149 were deemed inadmissible by the Board. In 264 cases, no offence or breach of discipline was identified. Happily, though, a staggering 31 cases out of the 689 actually processed by the Board in 2002 were resolved 'informally'. Fifteen minor breaches of discipline were referred to the Garda Commissioner, and 16 breaches of discipline were referred to a Tribunal for ultimate adjudication. So a total of a mere 4.5 per cent of *all* cases processed by the Board in 2002 were deemed worthy of attention at either Commissioner or Tribunal level.

Now either Irish people are incredibly fond of making large numbers of flimsy, unsubstantiated complaints against members of the Gardaí every year, or there is something seriously wrong with the structure and processes of the Board and the criteria by which they decide on the admissibility or otherwise of the complaints made. If the latter is the case, as I would suggest it is, it seems to support the now widely held public view that Gardaí operate in a self-policing, accountability-free environment, and that this disillusionment on the part of the public with the attitude of the Gardaí extends to a belief that they are not doing enough to combat crime on a street level. And whilst I'm not saying the Board doesn't carry out its duties with anything other than professionalism and diligence, its own Chairman, in his introduction to the annual report for

2002, states that it is not a perfect system by any means, and he suggests a few initiatives that could go some way to improving the situation. These include compelling Gardaí to 'answer questions for the purposes of any investigation', along with the recommendation that 'whatever body succeeds the Board, it should be given the teeth to carry out an independent investigation of its own and thus to enjoy public confidence'. He goes on to make the point that the current legislation has let the Board down, in that 'its total failure to give the Board the necessary powers with which to investigate matters and follow up those investigations, has prevented the Board from being a more effective body than it is'.

Another body set up to tackle a different group of baddies is the Criminal Assets Bureau. Its annual report for 2002 throws up some interesting facts as well. For the year ended 31 December 2002, the total cost of running the Bureau for the year was €5,401,284, and it collected a total of €10,003,816, out of a total of €12,830,763 that it demanded. €13 million isn't exactly chump change, and gives some idea of the scale of criminal activity going on in the country. Whatever amounts of monies the boys manage to collect are only a fraction of the total amount of funds being generated by the gangsters involved in drug trafficking, prostitution, people trafficking and the like. Take the drugs scene, for example. Every time somebody pays for a little bag of cocaine, factored in to the price is an amount to compensate Mr Big for the odd seizure that the boys make and the subsequent loss of working capital suffered by Mr Big.

McDonald's use the same system in all their restaurants.

I used to work in McDonald's franchise when I was in first year in college, and was instructed in the fine art of how to maximise profits by only keeping a certain amount of product in the heated 'bin' at any one time, this amount varying with the time of day and the day itself. All the food items in the bin had a certain life, and if not sold within that timeframe, were thrown in a waste bin. The contents of these waste bins were counted and noted every night, and over a period of time management were thus able to compensate themselves for losing the cost price of each product discarded by factoring into the retail price a waste margin. I'm not suggesting for one minute that the scumbags in the drug importation and distribution business in Ireland have their pricing strategies fine-tuned to such an extent as this, but I'm sure they take account of seizures to some degree. They probably even rig a few seizures deliberately to throw the boys off the scent, letting them catch a car with a kilo in it and then roll by in a forty-foot laden with the real deal while the boys are busy banging up some patsy. By the way, with €3,503,482, or 65 per cent, of its budget going on pay, this equated to an annual gross salary of some €66,100 for each of the 53 staff the Bureau employed. Nice work if you can get it, as they say.

Whatever about the current levels of crime in Ireland, it looks like they are set to rise still further if Dick's research is anything to go on. His findings indicate that crimes against society increase when there is a particular group in that society who feel oppressed, marginalised or disconnected from the levels of prosperity and progress enjoyed by the majority of the society in question. And if one thing's for sure, we've definitely got a lot of that kind of thing going on. Stats aren't worth a damn at the end of the day really, I suppose. If people don't *feel* safe in their beds or out on the streets, any kind of gloss or spin you try to put on them just ain't gonna wash. What might wash though is the sight of the 2,000 extra Gardaí that were 'promised' in the run-up to the last election. For the hell of it, here's one last statistic to finish up with. Between 2001 and 2003, some 430,000 members of the public were victims of a crime. That's a significant percentage of the population. And lots of them can vote.

Freedom and moral values

I suppose when compared to totally screwed-up kips like Afghanistan and those sorts of places, you'd have to say that we are more or less free to go about our business here. And I suppose we are free to hold whatever moral values we feel drawn to, though it would be nice if our duly elected elders and betters saw fit to lead by example and cling to a few of the most basic ones pertaining to what even a five-year-old would know as right and wrong. As Dick says, 'people are happier and better able to function when they feel they can trust other people.'

So our freedom itself is not under threat from a government point of view. It is quite possibly under threat though from ourselves and our peer groups as we all seem to be content to row in behind the prevailing ideology of the day that we should grab as much as we can as quickly as we can and to hell with everybody else.

Dick also notes that when asked the question, 'Would you say that most people can be trusted?', in 1959, 56 per cent of people in the UK said yes. By 1995 this figure was down to 31 per cent. In the US, people are regularly asked if they feel that people live 'as good lives – honest and moral – as they used to'. In 1952, 50 per cent thought that they did. By 1998 the corresponding figure was 25 per cent. I'm sure that were the same questions posed to a representative sample of Irish people, the answers would not unduly skew the results found in the UK or the US to any great degree.

Basically, what seems to have happened is that the relentless pursuit of economic development at any cost undertaken by governments has filtered down to an individual level to the extent that people see nothing wrong with pursuing their own interests at the expense of others. As for the solution to reversing this trend? That's a whole other book. One which I have no intention of even considering writing.

Just in case any of you feel miffed at the stall I set out above and point to the findings of any of the raft of other life/work satisfaction surveys carried out on both a national and pan-European level, can I just say that my pal Dick is interested in changes in levels of happiness over a *long* period of time, like a generation or so, and not just from year to year. Things don't change too much in a year, really, and if they do take a turn for the worst, people are likely to optimistically put that down to a blip and assume things will bounce back soon enough, and consequently don't let it colour their opinions too much. Life is long, not short, and apart from the fact that there is very little to be learned from conducting surveys on an annual basis, I would also question the quantity, construction and depth of the questions put to respondents in such surveys because of the time constraints such measures would place on those responsible for carrying out the survey.

Not saying that the Eurobarometer survey is carried out in a haphazard fashion or anything like that, but one I read there a while back in March seemed to have a lot of contradictions in it. For instance, the survey declares that we drink twice as much as the average European, that we ingest more amphetamines and ecstasy than any other European nation and that 86 per cent of us claim to eat a healthy balanced diet. However, the survey also reveals that 12 per cent of women and 14 per cent of men are clinically obese, that 54 per cent of us are overweight and that we consume the third highest amount of calories per day of any European country. Also, the average Irish adult watches 20 hours of television every week, something that's particularly terrifying when you consider that most of that 20 hours is probably spent watching soap after soap in half-hour segments, avidly devouring every last detail of the woes of a motley assortment of pathetic fictitious characters instead of examining their own lives and trying to figure out what's going on. Having said that, the escapism from such navel gazing and examination this telly ogling affords us is probably why so many people religiously keep up to speed with the goings-on in the lives of Roy and Hayley and Cat and Alfie and whoever else they can squeeze in to their sofa schedule.

We also have the latest average retirement age in the EU, at 63.1 years, and our life expectancy is the lowest in the EU, at 73 years for men and 78.5 years for women. And during those extra working years we apparently work longer hours per week than many others, 37.2 per week as compared to 35 for our friends north of the border, with 40 per cent of people saying that they feel stressed, and many others complaining that they are too tired to enjoy life after work to the extent that they would like to. Then 90 per cent of us turn around and say that we are generally satisfied with our jobs, with two-thirds of us adding that they would continue to work even if they were rich enough not to have to work.

In another survey, only 2 per cent of respondents declared that they had a great deal of confidence in government; government in general that is, I regret to add, not just the shower that are wrongfully occupying the corridors of power at the moment. This lack of confidence in government mustn't be that deep-rooted, though, because when we get a chance to do something about it, the Irish electorate has one of the worst turnout rates for national parliamentary elections in the EU, the fourth lowest. No wonder Paddy Power have installed those goons as the firm favourites to regain office in the next general election, giving them odds of 1/10 after the last Ard Fheis.

Forty per cent of Europeans identify exclusively with their own nationality; in Ireland the figure is 49 per cent, and yet only the people of Luxembourg apparently have more enthusiasm for the EU than ourselves.

None of that makes a whole lot of sense to me, to be honest with you. On the face of it, it would appear that either we have deficiently selective and very short-term memories or have absolutely no qualms about lying to the people charged with carrying out the research that forms the basis of the results revealed in such surveys. Either way, I think it shows that they have to be taken with a pinch of salt, in that they are highly quantitative and closed-ended and only solicit people's opinions on their level of satisfaction with their everyday lives in relation to how they felt about the same thing a relatively short time previously.

Anyway, I'm sure you've had it up to here (I'm gesturing to my eyes) with stats and facts, so I'll move on. What's the point of all this painstaking, long-term research at the end of the day? Well, Dick has proposed a rather radical solution: how about governments scale back their long-held and rather blinkered view that adopting policies solely on their potential to create economic growth is the way to go, promoting as it does a culture of self-interest, distrust, and insecurity, and focus instead on creating and nurturing an environment where the factors universally acknowledged as being central to people's happiness in the long term take centre stage?

Wishful thinking? On the notion of its validity, I think not. On the chances of them ever actually deigning to adopt such an approach, I fear yes, it is wishful thinking. The reason for this is that even though it is obvious to any right-thinking Irish citizen possessed of the most basic cognitive faculties that the function of government is to enrich the nation as a whole and provide the infrastructural societal foundation upon which every citizen can individually build a fulfilled life, rich with purpose and meaning, some day achieving a state of mind that could only be described as happiness, a cursory glance at the nation as we find it today would show that not only has the government failed to do that which they are elected and therefore compelled to do, but that they frequently display astounding levels of arrogance in utterly disregarding the wishes of their employers – us.

You know that old saying, 'It's the economy, stupid'? Might I suggest an amendment to our elected representatives that could be of use to them, just in case they ever deign to try and figure out what's making so many people so unhappy?

'It's not *just* the economy, stupid!'

Epilogue

Flashback to 6 May 2002.

In government, Fianna Fáil will permanently end waiting lists in our hospitals within two years through a combination of bed capacity, primary care, secondary care and targeted reform initiatives.

No, it's not an excerpt from a satirical sketch, but a quote from Fianna Fáil's last election manifesto. Two-and-a-half years have since passed. Have waiting lists been abolished? No. Figures compiled by the Minister's own department some time ago revealed that there were in excess of 27,000 people on waiting lists for medical treatment. More terrifying is the realisation that the figures show a decrease of only about 7 per cent on the previous year.

If we take an election manifesto at face value, it could be likened to a promise, made to the electorate by a political party, swearing faithfully to perform certain tasks once they have been installed in government. When you place your trust in someone and they break that trust by failing to fulfil a promise made, you would, quite rightly, be decidedly more wary of trusting them when they next called upon your trust, particularly when their inability to fulfil the promise made was shown to have been wide of the mark by 93 per cent.

Of course, this being Ireland, there are actually two waiting lists. The first is the one the Department of Health refers to. The second waiting list is comprised of those people waiting to get on the waiting list, and is estimated to be about four times as long as the first list. This is because to get on the Department's waiting list, you must first get an appointment with a consultant, something which can take months, and in some cases, years, to achieve.

But even when you manage to secure your place on the official waiting list, at say, number 27,324, your troubles are far from over, because when your number finally comes up, chances are there won't even be a bed for you. One patient in the north-west region who was suspected of having cancer, had an operation to ascertain his prognosis cancelled four times in the space of a few months because there was no bed available in Dublin for him.

It is estimated that some 20 per cent of available beds in Dublin hospitals, about 600 in all, are occupied by 'bed-blockers', as they are affectionately known. These patients have nowhere else to go for post-operative step-down care, and so remain in acute wards in hospitals at a cost of €6,000 a week, according to the Irish Hospitals Consultants Association (IHCA). The required level of care for these patients could be found in a nursing home for less than €1,000 a week. So it would seem that a solution of sorts could be found in the outsourcing of post-operative care to the private sector, principally in nursing homes. But no, that won't work, because even with the three area health boards in the eastern region having 1,589 partially funded beds and 1,412 fully funded beds in private nursing homes at their disposal, it has been said that the Eastern Regional Health Authority (ERHA) have in fact cancelled a number of contract beds in nursing homes. Why? To reduce costs. The result? Instances like the one where a patient in a Dublin hospital who was fit for discharge after seven days, remained in hospital for a further 240 days because there was apparently nowhere else for him to go.

Have you been up around Ballymun lately? The whole place is undergoing quite a transformation, and not before time too. One of the cornerstones of the redevelopment of the area was the construction of one of the largest community health centres ever built in the State, designed to accommodate the needs of over 100,000 people living north of the city. The building was completed well over a year ago, but has yet to open its doors to the community it was built for. It cost €56 million to build, but lies idle because the relevant health authorities have not given the green light for the €3.5 million fitting-out costs to be spent. The current centre is woefully ill-equipped to accommodate the population base it serves. In the past the centre has been closed on health and safety grounds, baby clinics have been cancelled because of the freezing temperatures in the place, and doctors have been unable to access computerised patient records because of power failures. These totally unacceptable inadequacies all put pressure on the local accident and emergency units in surrounding hospitals because there is nowhere else for patients to go. This gives rise to overcrowding, which forces the hospitals to cancel elective surgery operations. On one day alone last year, it was reported that over 100 elective operations due to be performed in Dublin hospitals were cancelled as a result of overcrowding.

As if that kind of thing wasn't bad enough, the management at these same hospitals have been told to reduce their costs, resulting in some drastic measures being proposed in order to comply with the minister's instructions. Early last year, for instance, the management at Beaumont Hospital was told to reduce its costs by 10 per cent in order to save €20 million. Already stretched to the limit in its efforts to provide the highest levels of patient care, this demand led management and the ERHA to suggest the following measures: shut down 35 beds, discontinue the use of a number of medical devices, eliminate the overnight dialysis shift, and place a limit on the amount of cancer and dialysis treatment carried out.

Where does it all end? In a two-tier society such as ours, the people at the thin end of the wedge and most in need of an efficient and progressive health service, continue to suffer. Those at the fat end of the wedge are fleeing the public system and opting for private health care, something evidenced by the fact that the promoters behind the Blackrock Clinic are well advanced in their expansion plans, with more operators sure to follow suit. This flight of the haves and have-lots would seem to suit the government perfectly. It doesn't want to raise the taxes that are needed for investment in the public services because this would upset their friends and those in the middle and upper classes who tend to vote in higher numbers than the have-nots on low pay who live in disadvantaged areas. So the more people that opt for private healthcare, the more the pressure on the public system is alleviated, and the more reports can be generated to justify further downgrades and reduced investment. And the more the poor get less. But fuck them: they don't even vote.

In January 2003 pupils attending Ringaskiddy National School were told to remain indoors during lunchtimes on windy days in case they were injured by slates falling from the roof of the 105-year-old building. Its three classrooms and two prefabs accommodate 90 pupils. Dehumidifiers are left on constantly in the damp rooms and the school has no running water. In October 2003, it was reported that pupils in St Brendan's primary school in Blennerville in Tralee, Co. Kerry, were told not to attend for classes due to a problem with rat infestation. A new school was apparently promised three years previously but was not delivered due to funding cuts. St Safan's National School in Castlefin, Co. Donegal, was promised funding would be made available for certain health and safety refurbishments which were necessary to provide toilet facilities for a male student confined to a wheelchair. Whenever he needs to use the toilet, a staff member has to ring his home and ask his father to come down and bring him home. In Gallbhaile National School in Galbally, Enniscorthy, Co. Wexford, the government would rather pay for the students to drink Ballygowan mineral water than provide funding for a new water treatment system.

In the primary school sector alone, the Irish National Teachers Organisation (INTO) estimates there are at least 400 such sorry tales to be told the length and breadth of the country. In December of 2003, while announcing to a room full of cameras some highlights from his plans for 2004, the Minister for Education and Science, Noel Dempsey, declared that some €387 million would be spent on 170 different school building projects in an effort to address the disastrous accommodation situation and other problems. While that might sound like a lot of money, it represents less than 10 per cent of the €5 billion euro budget the minister had to spend. Also, in what was terrifyingly described as an 'initiative', the minister proudly announced that 2004 heralded the first school to be constructed using a newly developed standardised design. Haven't they come a long way?

Whilst making the spending announcements, the minister also reiterated his belief that 'devolving funding, responsibility and authority to schools to the greatest extent possible is the way forward'. Why wouldn't he, when such a strategy abdicates him from taking the rap for any number of the myriad problems that beset the education system? For instance, when confronted with the issue of rat-infested prefabs at Meánscoil an Leith-Triúigh in Cloghane, on the Dingle peninsula in Kerry, the minister said, 'I do not accept any school should be infested with rats or mice, something that should be easily resolved. The school board of management should make sure it is.' On another occasion, with an announcement worthy of a geeky conspiracy theorist, the minister actually suggested that some school boards were deliberately allowing their building to fall into disrepair in order to pressurise the department into allocating them increased funding, saying 'I am not aware of rats running up and down the corridor in schools. That is bad management.' (I wonder if he thinks Lee Harvey Oswald acted alone?) Newsflash Noelie: you're the managing director, the buck starts and stops with you.

On 18 April of this year I clicked on to the Department of Education website to see if I could find out some more about the school-building programme. I followed a few links and arrived at:

http://www.education.ie/home/home.jsp?maincat=17216 &category=22136&feature=04_sch_building_programme &sectionpage=&language=EN&link=&page=1 only to be told 'Sorry, there was no content found for this section'. I sincerely hope that this was the result of some technological gremlins at work. Otherwise, kids, you're all screwed.

Similar to the health service, the education sector has evidenced a flight of the haves and have-lots in recent years, with affluent parents topping up the education their children get in school with expensive private tutoring and intensive revision courses in private institutes. This results in greater inequities as those from disadvantaged areas are squeezed out of higher education.

These two areas, health and education, are without doubt two of the most critical to discuss when examining the state of a nation. That's precisely why I haven't done so. I am not sufficiently equipped to do so, nor do I have the heart to do so. The more I looked for information on the subjects at the outset of writing this book, the quicker I came to the conclusion that anything I did write would be inconclusive and only raise more questions than I could have any hope of answering. If that sounds like a cop-out, well and good. At least it's an honest cop-out. I don't have any kids, so I don't know what it's like to have to walk up to an antiquated health centre to get them injected against something, only to find that it's been closed because of a power shortage. I don't know what it's like to have to watch children fall behind in their education because the school they attend cannot provide as good an education as that afforded to children attending private schools. And that's that.

Have you ever seen that movie *Network*? No? Thought not. Peter Finch, in an amazing performance, plays a seriously pissed-off, world-weary newscaster by the name of Howard Beale, who gets to the stage where he just can't take it anymore. Fed up with all the bullshit propaganda spewed out by the media about the way things are, he decides to tell it like it is one night on his regular newscast. It's a great scene, one of the best you're ever gonna see, and I feel compelled to reprint Howard Beale's shining moment of glory here now for your pleasure, because if I sat at this laptop for the next month – which I can't because I was supposed to have this book finished last week – I couldn't come up with anything better.

I don't have to tell you things are bad. Everybody knows things are bad. It's a depression. Everybody's out of work or scared of losing their job, the dollar buys a nickel's worth, banks are going bust, shopkeepers keep a gun under the counter, punks are running wild in the streets, and there's nobody anywhere who seems to know what to do, and there's no end to it. We know the air's unfit to breathe and our food is unfit to eat, and we sit and watch our TVs while some local newscaster tells us today we had fifteen homicides and sixty-three violent crimes, as if that's the way it's supposed to be. We all know things are bad. Worse than bad. They're crazy. It's like everything's going crazy. So we don't go out anymore. We sit in the house, and slowly the world we live in gets smaller, and all we ask is, please, at least leave us alone in our living rooms. Let me have my toaster and my TV and my steel-belted radials, and I won't say anything, just leave us alone. Well, I'm not going to leave you alone. I want you to get mad.

I don't want you to riot. I don't want you to protest. I don't want you to write to your congressman, because I wouldn't know what to tell you to write. I don't know what to do about the depression and the inflation and the defence budget and the Russians and the crime in the street. All I know is first you got to get mad. You've got to say: 'I'm mad as hell and I'm not going to take this anymore. I'm a human being, goddammit. My life has value.' So I want you to get up now. I want you to get out of your chairs and go to the window. I want you to go to the window, open it, stick your head out and yell. I want you to yell: 'I'm mad as hell and I'm not going to take this anymore!'

Get up from your chairs. Go to the window. Open it. Stick your head out and yell, and keep yelling.

First you have to get mad. When you're mad enough we'll figure out what to do about the depression and the inflation and the oil crisis. Things have got to change. But you can't change unless you're mad. You have to get mad. Go to the window, stick your head out and yell. I want you to yell: 'I'm mad as hell and I'm not going to take this anymore!'

Brilliant, isn't it? And would you believe that that was written by a man called Paddy Chayefsky nearly thirty years ago, in 1976? And yet, by and large, everything Howard Beale said way back then, could just as easily be said here today in Dublin. It could. And it needs to be said. (I was only recently informed that Frank McDonald quoted some of the above lines in his book *The Destruction of Dublin* some years ago. Fair play, Frank, on the ball and all that, but I haven't actually read that particular book, and consequently take full credit for what I thought was an original idea to include it here.)

All the same, though, now that I think about it, given the state of things in this country, I'm not sure that going to your window and shouting, 'I'm mad as hell and I'm not going to take this anymore!' is the best thing to do, because as the litany of U-turns and broken promises made by Bertie & Co. surely attest to, if there's one thing we know for sure, it's that nobody in the government is listening to you and me and what we think about the way things are and the way they should be.

* * *

It's a complicated business, this publishing thing. Writing the book itself is only half the job. As soon as I finish the main text, it goes to the publishers where some poor unfortunate sod has to take my rambling mess and put some kind of coherent structure on it. Then it comes back to me all nicely double-spaced and paginated so that when the lawyers grill me on the many potentially libellous things I have said about various people who would ordinarily view themselves as decent, hardworking pillars of the community, we're all reading from the same page, literally. I then back up what I've said with supporting documentation, both factual and fabricated, to see how much I can get past them. (Had a hit rate of about 85 per cent this time – pretty good going I thought.) After I've made the necessary changes to avert the threat of litigation, the text gets prettied up a little more before going off to be typeset, something which takes ages because even in these technologically advanced days, it requires hours and hours of man/woman-hours. Around this time the marketing gang do up the jacket (cover to you and me). As is my wont, I object to the proposed cover, normally on very petty grounds, but nonetheless it holds us up another bit, until such time as it's agreed upon. The sales reps start spreading the word to the trade on their rounds, the marketing guys devise a marketing campaign, and the PR gang decide on how best to 'package' me and my tome for the media thing. Eventually, the proofs arrive – a printout of how the physical book will look – and this is my last chance to make 'minor' alterations to the text before saying goodbye to it forever and waiting for it to appear in bookshops the length and breadth of the country.

This is the stage I am now at, on a Friday night when I should be out having a few beers and not chatting up cute chicks. Given the supposedly contemporaneous nature of the book, the whole snapshot-type this-is-how-things-are vibe I was going for as I prattled on about this and that, it's only natural that as I frittered away my advance on a very enjoyable tour of the west coast of France there have been a number of developments in the various areas I have cursorily covered in the book, which means that on top of making minor corrections to the text in an effort to make it more readable, I am also burdened with the task of having to update some of these areas in another effort to retain whatever currency the book might have. The professional approach to take with such a task would be to go back over the whole text and rework it to incorporate these developments, but seeing as how I'm not that professional, I have instead opted for a postscript type of approach, where I will very quickly run through a few things and add another two cents to the two cents I have already posited, giving you a total of four cents worth of my opinions on the state of the nation, and all for only €10.99. Where would you get it?

The Drink Thing

I sold my taxi plate a couple of months ago so I've no recent first-hand accounts of drunken debauchery or alcohol-fuelled violence on the streets, but I'm content enough to suggest that depending on whether you're a scumbag or a decent enough individual, partaking in, or avoiding getting unwittingly caught up in a fracas of some description is still part and parcel of going out on a Saturday night, despite what Mickey Mac would have you believe. I heard him on the *The Last Word* the other day, modestly taking all the credit for the alleged significant reductions in public order offences over the last while. In fairness to him, all he had to support his assertions were a load of bullshit stats generated from official sources, and if there's two things I know, it's that, firstly, you can prove anything on paper, and secondly, that a large proportion of the drink-related public order offences which appear to be of huge concern to the minister are committed by young people. As I said before, it has been suggested that as many as one in three crimes committed against those aged 25 and under go unreported, and I would think it's safe to say that the majority of the perpetrators of crimes against under-25s are themselves under-25s, and that excessive alcohol consumption plays a large part in these offences.

To this end, might I suggest to the minister that some Saturday night he arrange for his driver to collect him from his elegant home in Ranelagh about midnight and take him on a little tour of Dublin city centre so that he can more accurately gauge for himself the reality of the situation?

Furthermore, might I also suggest that he get his own house in order as well and rectify the situation where he and his Oireachtas colleagues have been supping pints in the bar in Dáil Éireann for years when the place appears not to have had a licence? Under the current legislation, of which the Minister for Justice is the guardian, the Oireachtas must apply to the courts for a liquor licence like any other publican. In the course of its application, an applicant must demonstrate that he or she is of good character, and that the venue in question is a fit location for alcohol to be served. Don't fancy their chances, to be honest with you.

The Infrastructure Thing
Aye, aye, aye. I'm sorry I ever covered this topic – the bloody mess just gets worse and worse, with no satisfactory end in sight. So the Luas is up and running. Big deal, you'd swear we'd invented the wheel. The Paris metro progressed from foundations to opening in 20 *months*, without anything like the plant and machinery the Railway Procurement Agency (RPA) had at its disposal. When? At the beginning of the 1900s.

In an effort to coerce people into buying weekly and monthly commuter tickets, each platform at each station is equipped with only two ticket-vending machines, resulting in delays as people queue to buy a ticket. And after all the time and money spent on the thing, the supposedly high-tech, ultra modern trams aren't even equipped with ticket validation machines like the ones on the buses. And because of the prohibitive cost of employing actual humans to validate tickets, the whole operation is being run on an 'honour system', as a senior RPA director euphemistically put it. What a joke.

Do you remember your man I mentioned before, Mr Donal Mangan, the former acting chief executive of the RPA, whose job was advertised without his prior consultation. Two years after initiating legal action over the affair, Mr Mangan settled his action with the state for close on €1 million.

Essentially the Luas is a typically Irish solution – too little, too late, and too expensive. As the Madrid metro's director of projects and works, Ildefonso de Matias Jimenez, on a visit to Dublin a while back with Professor Manuel Melis Maynar, the president of the Madrid metro network, said, 'Really your Luas is a toy train more or less.'

And as for the proposed metro system to link the city centre to Dublin airport, I don't know what the story is now, mainly because the people in charge of deciding if, when and how it is to be built don't themselves know what the story is. Every time they're pressed on the issue, they trot out the same meaningless patter, inevitably finishing their sentences with 'shortly', 'in the coming weeks', 'next month' or 'in due course'. They've been doing this for years now, and the irony is that whilst they always claim to have the interests of the taxpayer at heart when making decisions on projects of this nature, their legendary procrastination and bungling are themselves eventually significant contributing factors in the massive escalation in the costs of these projects, with such cost overruns being borne by the taxpayer.

In July of this year, I was trying to decipher what Bertie was saying when he was pressed on the metro issue in the Dáil, and from what I could make out, he seemed to be indicating that the project looked a bit pricey, saying that an integrated underground metro system for Dublin couldn't be given priority over other loftier goals. A week later though, Seamus Brennan told the Dáil that he expected the airport metro link to go ahead as there was a provision for it in the Programme for Government. Apparently, those clever fellas in the RPA had managed to fix the gremlins that were playing havoc with their financial modelling software and advised him that 'the total estimated direct capital cost of construction in 2002 prices is €1.2 billion'. I don't think so. Why use 2002 as your base year for calculations in the year 2004? Why not compound the 2004 costs by a factor approximating the likely increases in the relevant costs associated with the project and at least give some semblance of not taking everyone around you for a complete gobshite?

The port tunnel height debate still trundles on too, with the company carrying out the work saying that the design changes necessary to increase the operating height of the tunnel will cost between €30 million and €60 million to implement. The €30 million difference is apparently attributable to whether or not the alteration work would be carried out with or without a full project team. Nice work if you can get it.

I think some course of 'action' has been decided upon in

relation to the Red Cow roundabout, but I don't know what it is and I don't care, because I sincerely doubt that whatever belated half-baked idea is being proceeded with makes any provision for the likely increase in vehicle numbers in the coming years, with the result that the modifications made to the roundabout will not be adequate to cater for the demands placed on it. After all, the people in charge are the same morons who managed to miscalculate the cost of the national roads programme by almost €10 billion, and still haven't managed to deliver it, being three years behind schedule as things now stand.

The Property Thing

The property ownership epidemic sweeping the country shows no sign of abating, no doubt much to the continued delight of Messrs Whelan, Mennolly, Cotter and Dunne *et al* in the building game. I didn't bother looking for the latest figures from the Irish National Survey of Housing Quality, because I know that whatever the price of the average home in Dublin was six months ago when I first covered the topic, it's more than that now. Clearly, there is still huge demand for houses, particularly starter homes, and no doubt there are still plenty of developers out there hoarding vast tracts of lands until such time as they can maximise the profits to be made from developing residential units on them. In the Dáil in July of this year, the Minister of State for housing and urban renewal, Mr Noel Ahern, countered this suggestion when discussing the findings of a Goodbody report on the issue, before finishing off with a joke and claiming that housing today was only slightly less affordable than it was in 1992.

In a startling development during the year, Mr Ahern

also announced that landlords will be forced to register their rental properties with the relevant local authorities. The pathetic series of measures introduced to try and compel landlords to comply with the new legislation included bold measures such as a fine of €3,000 and/or up to six months in prison if convicted of the likes of failing to carry out essential repairs or neglecting a property. As a sop to interested parties, provision was also made for the establishment of a Residential Tenancies Board to consider complaints made by tenants against their profiteering landlords, a measure that has been consistently called for since 1999. Better late than never, I suppose.

On the numerous affordable housing 'initiatives' announced over the last while, I'm pleased to report that no further research on the subject was required by me. This is because nothing has been done to actually provide the houses that were promised, save for a few out in Finglas, which surprise, surprise, just happen to be in Noel Ahern's constituency. With up to 45 per cent of the cost of every house purchased going straight back to the government in the form of VAT, stamp duty and development levies, you'd think they'd get on with the building programme quick smart.

The Racism Thing
A quick scan through some of the papers would confirm that things are as bad as ever on the racism front, with almost daily reports of non-nationals being verbally and physically abused, sexually assaulted, harassed and discriminated against. Walk through certain quarters of any city in Ireland and you'll witness this kind of thing first-hand. What you do about it is another thing.

The Amnesty survey I referred to before was, you might

recall, conducted amongst a group of 600 individuals from a variety of ethnic backgrounds. Just for those of you out there who aren't too fond of the niggers and reckon that the respondents' non-national status may have coloured the findings of the survey, I just last week came across another survey on the Amnesty website, this time carried out amongst a representative group of thoroughbred potato-chomping Paddies, and the results weren't a whole lot different. Over half of those surveyed, 56 per cent, said they now considered racism to be a serious problem in Ireland, and only 26 per cent of them said that they believed the government was doing enough to combat the problem. As Amnesty puts it, 'The vacuum caused by the Government's inactivity on racism has led to dangerous levels of ignorance and confusion over asylum and immigration issues. The Government's own research – produced by its Know Racism campaign in 2004 – shows that one in five people in Ireland has witnessed a racist incident.'

Prior to the recent citizenship referendum, Colm Ó Cuanacháin, Secretary General of Amnesty International's Irish Section, commented that the 'absence of a proper Government anti-racism awareness campaign has left the referendum campaign in danger of possible abuse by candidates promoting racist policies, and by distributing racist material. We have already received reports of misleading campaign literature, and *are concerned that Government inaction on racism is feeding this ignorance.*' You saw yourself what happened there.

The Tribunals Thing

Well, Ray Burke pleaded guilty to the two offences he was charged with, and with any luck will be spending Christmas in jail looking for a file in a chocolate cake. The Flynn dynasty continue to beggar belief down in the castle, whilst no doubt lording it around Castlebar as if they're the most upstanding folk to be found. Lorcan Allen was suspended from the Fianna Fáil parliamentary party for forging Bertie's signature on a letter endorsing his local election campaign in Wexford. The chief superintendent in Gorey received a letter from Cork-based Dr Michael Grimes, requesting that a file on the matter be sent to the DPP, politely adding that, 'I look forward to visiting Mr Allen in jail in due course.' Maybe he could look in on Rambo while he's there – make sure he has enough soap.

As regards the golden circle thing, I was trawling through a few old Dáil debates last week trying to see if I could elaborate further on something I said about a particular individual on page 138. Unfortunately, seeing as how I am not afforded the same privilege that Dáil members enjoy in being able to say whatever they like about whomever they like whenever they like, I had to give it a miss, which is a pity, because that particular member, with numerous acolytes in tow, will next year be banging on doors all over Drumcondra in a bid to elicit support for his reelection to the Dáil so that the party of which he is currently leader can mismanage the state for another four years. What I can do, though, is refer you to the debate in question and suggest that you have a look at it when you get a minute. Or an hour, maybe. You'll find it at:

http://historical-debates.oireachtas.ie/D/0480/D.0480. 199709100014.html

It's kinda long, but it's actually hilarious when you get into it. The debate took place on 10 September 1997 and ostensibly concerned itself with the Report of the Tribunal of Inquiry (Dunnes Payments) and Establishment of Tribunal of Inquiry. The Taoiseach, Mr Ahern, made the usual impassioned speech about the need to root out corruption and what have you – must know it by heart at this stage – and a few of his lackeys then jumped up to trot out thinly veiled declarations of love and support for their glorious leader. The opposition parties got their turn and used the occasion to recap on some of the scandals that beset previous Fianna Fáil administrations, of which Bertie was a prominent member, and about which he must have known a lot more than he chooses to let on. All the old favourites are there.

There's the beef export credit insurance fiasco, where £200 million of public money was jeopardised in order to underwrite beef deals with Iraq, and the way the IDA was unlawfully pressurised to help Larry Goodman. There's the sale of 147 acres at Glending Woods to Cement Roadstone Holdings (CRH) for only £1.25 million. There's the passport for investment thing, the unusual sale of Carysfort college to UCD, and of course, there's the Telecom affair.

You'll laugh. You'll cry. You'll have steam coming out your ears.

The Happiness Thing
Are you happy?

* * *

That's definitely it. As of today, Thursday, 29 July 2004, I couldn't care less what developments arise in any of the areas I have covered. Think I'll book a flight somewhere. Good luck.